Anglican Re-Formation

Anglican Re-Formation

Jack Estes

WIPF & STOCK · Eugene, Oregon

ANGLICAN RE-FORMATION

Copyright © 2017 Jack Estes. All rights reserved. Except for brief quotations in critical publications or reviews, no part of this book may be reproduced in any manner without prior written permission from the publisher. Write: Permissions, Wipf and Stock Publishers, 199 W. 8th Ave., Suite 3, Eugene, OR 97401.

Wipf & Stock
An Imprint of Wipf and Stock Publishers
199 W. 8th Ave., Suite 3
Eugene, OR 97401

www.wipfandstock.com

PAPERBACK ISBN: 978-1-4982-0741-6
HARDCOVER ISBN: 978-1-4982-0743-0
EBOOK ISBN: 978-1-4982-0742-3

Manufactured in the U.S.A.   APRIL 25, 2017

All scripture quotations, unless otherwise indicated, are taken from the The Holy Bible, English Standard Version® (ESV®) Copyright © 2001 by Crossway, a publishing ministry of Good News Publishers. All rights reserved

Dedicated to my loving wife,
Jenny
With thanksgiving for her faithful support
and encouragement along the way

Contents

List of Illustrations | *viii*
Preface | *ix*
Acknowledgments | *xi*
Thesis | *xiii*
Introduction | *xv*

1. Anglican-Ism | 1
2. Paradigm to Paradigm | 22
3. Two Visions | 38
4. Crisis | 55
5. Anglican Re-Formation | 71
6. The Anglican World | 87

Appendix I: The Chicago-Lambeth Quadrilateral 1886, 1888 | *91*
Appendix II: Anglican-Ism | *94*
Bibliography | *101*

Illustrations

0.1 *Ink and quill*; ClipartOf.com/1157541COLLCO178 | xii
0.2 *Celtic cross*; © Sergey Galushko / Dreamstime.com | xiv
1.1 *Compass rose* | 1
1.2 *Via Media*; © Jack Estes | 7
1.3 © Jack Estes | 19
2.1 *Past, Present, Future*; © Richard Thomas / Dreamstime.com | 22
2.2 © Jack Estes | 26
2.3 *Premodern, Modern, Postmodern*; © Mel Chua, http://blog.melchua.com/2014/05/16/postmodernism-in-a-3-panel-comic/ | 30
2.4 *Scientific Cartoon—In the middle ages*; www.cartoonstock.com (shm1153) | 32
3.1 *Two visions*; © iStock.com/skodonnell | 38
4.1 *Frayed rope*; © iStock.com/DNY59 | 55
5.1 *Haystack*; © Lilittas1 / Dreamstime.com | 71
6.1 *The Anglican World*; © Anglican Communion | 87

Preface

Dear Reader,

Thank you for your interest in *Anglican Re-Formation*. Certainly, we are living through a very dynamic time in the history of the Anglican Church and the world in general. What follows are my thoughts on how we as Anglicans, and as Christians, can engage with the current situation that we find ourselves in and lay a new foundation for the future.

Fr. Jack Estes
St. Luke's Anglican Church
2801 Bernard Street, Bakersfield, CA 93306
stlukesbak@gmail.com

Acknowledgments

Throughout these past seasons as I have been working on this manuscript, I have discovered a truth. There is much more to publishing a book than simply writing it. The process begins as an idea, which then grows into a vision. In order to bring the vision into being, writing is just the first stage. Next, comes the rewriting, editing, honing, that in end result in a book actually becoming a book.

As a writer, I wish to humbly give thanks to those who have patiently assisted me with this process. These are my family, friends, and colleagues who brought their gifts and energy alongside me in order to complete the task:

Jenny Estes
> Editing of word choice and reflections on spiritual content

Janelle Eastridge
> Editing in grammar, punctuation and plot flow

Shirley Hessler
> Computer expertise: illustrations, webpage and Facebook

The Congregation of St. Luke's Anglican Church, Bakersfield, CA
> Steadfast encouragement and prayer

Thank you to all above. It is my hope that you will share in the fulfillment of God's purposes for this manuscript. I pray God will bless you in bringing your own visions into being as well.

"It is not real until it is written"
—FR. JACK ESTES

Thesis

The Anglican Communion is uniquely poised to proclaim the gospel and to expand the Kingdom of God in the twenty-first century. In order to affect this proclamation, the immediate crisis of vision, structure, and leadership must be acknowledged and overcome. Essentially, a re-formation is needed which provides for a fresh commitment to Biblical truth and practice, while uniting Anglicans in common purpose and polity.

Anglican Re-Formation examines the underlying principles of the Anglican expression of Christian faith, and how they have interacted with the historical paradigm shifts of, first, Western society, and, now, the Global Village. Taken together with an analysis of the theological dynamics of the present crisis, *Re-Formation* continues with a number of proposals intended to encourage the communion forward into a place of vibrant worship and witness throughout the world.

Re-Formation
"The action or process of forming again"

—MERRIAM-WEBSTER

Introduction

The Anglican Communion is at a crossroads. We have reached the tipping point on the fulcrum, where things can no longer be kept in balance. The decisions made now will affect not only the future direction of Anglicanism, but also the very foundations of Anglican belief. A choice must be made between two competing worldviews, which are at heart radically different. Which foundation shall we chose to build upon? What will the faith of future Anglicans look like? Will there even be an Anglican church, or will the whole thing simply unravel?

The cataclysmic events now taking place in the Anglican Communion represent a microcosm in the state of Christianity as a whole. The same dynamics which fuel the fires of the current Anglican angst smolder beneath the surface of worldwide Christianity, as we move into the twenty-first century. The church universal is facing a polarization between the traditional Christian faith and a revised,

INTRODUCTION

progressive "Christianity" that is in fact nothing short of a new religious movement. Christians of every denomination must choose between the two. The foundational principles and theology of each are radically different. They cannot be reconciled: Traditional vs. Progressive; Liberal vs. Orthodox; Old vs. New; however one makes the distinction we have come to a point of decision.

The time has come for all who would call themselves Christians, to decide which set of beliefs and practices will be adhered to and taught in the church, and which vision will be offered to the world as the Christian faith. Are we sinners brought back into relationship with God through the atoning sacrifice of Jesus Christ, or, are all made in the image of God and therefore inherently good? Is Jesus Christ the only means of salvation, or, is salvation available through a plurality of religions that lead us to the knowledge of the divine presence within each person?

While living in and through this historical context, much of the Christian church retains a commitment to the faith once delivered to the saints. Across denominational lines, the "orthodox" hold fast to the belief in an objective authority of the Bible, the transcendent nature of God, and the need for regeneration of sinful human nature. Rather than being informed by the prevailing winds of postmodernity and the directives of liberal theology, many Anglicans, Catholics, and Protestants continue to teach and confess the traditional principles and theology which have been the bedrock of the faith for two thousand years.

Writing from the midst of the struggles of the Anglican Church, I seek to ignite not only a re-formation of the Anglican Communion, but a global reunification and revival of the Christian church. In the crisis we are facing, I see a historic opportunity for Christianity as a whole. As the tapestry that was once the Anglican Church unravels, I see the possibilities of the bonding together of a new, unified, Fellowship of the Christian Church worldwide.

Yet, I must confess to a sense of urgency, as the shift to a new era has already begun. We must act, and act soon, or it may well be too late.

—Fr. Jack Estes

Ism:
"A distinctive doctrine, cause, or theory;
The adherence to a system or class of principles"
—MERRIAM WEBSTER

Chapter 1
Anglican-Ism

The Anglican Church is a world-wide phenomena, with thirty-nine provinces spanning the globe, hundreds of bishops and archbishops, and millions of faithful members. As far as Christian denominations are concerned, the Anglican Communion ranks third in strength worldwide, eclipsed only by the Eastern Orthodox Churches and the mammoth Roman Catholic Church led by the pope in Rome. Yet, what exactly is the Anglican-Ism? Ask the question to a room full of Anglicans, and you will probably hear a room full of answers. Ask the question to those outside the Anglican fold, and you may not find any answer that is coherent. To quote a phrase, it's complicated. The answer lies in considering the essential principles on which the Anglican Church was founded to begin with, along with the ongoing historical developments and decisions which have added to its character. Of course, such an undertaking could easily fill several volumes, and what I offer here is more of an astute, succinct assessment for the purpose of this book. Nevertheless, let us consider the following as pieces to the puzzle from which, when properly fit together, emerge a portrait of the Anglican-Ism:

> The Church of England—Cranmer and Henry VIII
> Protestant and Catholic Spirituality
> The Via Media
> Early Apologists
> —Jewel and Hooker
> Anglican Comprehensiveness
> —The Evangelical Revival and the Oxford Movement
> Autonomous Fellowship
> Chicago-Lambeth Quadrilateral
> The Big Tent

Church of England

The Anglican Reformation—Sixteenth Century

In order to arrive at a coherent discussion of the Anglican re-formation of the present day, we must first begin with a consideration of the Anglican reformation of the 16th century-a reformation that was in and of itself part of the larger protestant movement of the time. For it was in this period of time that foundational principles were established in Anglicanism which continue to exert influence down through time and into the present. For our purposes, we will not attempt an exhaustive analysis of the protestant reformation. However, certain key elements that formed the distinctively Anglican expression are necessary to identify and explore, so that when we arrive at the discussion of present day reformation we may understand the theological and ecclesiological landscape in which we live. Specifically, then, let us consider: the conflict between protestant and catholic spirituality; the solution of the Via Media; apologists Jewel and Hooker; and the Anglican comprehensiveness that developed as a result.

Protestant and Catholic Spirituality

Spirituality in the broad sense of the word may be best understood as our whole approach to relationship with God. In this sense spirituality includes theology, the understanding of who God is, worship, both corporate and private, revelation, how God communicates, and especially authority, that is what we deem to be authoritative in our spiritual lives. In the sixteenth century, theology, worship, revelation, and authority combined to form the matrix of the conflict between protestant and catholic factions within the church: each assumed different approaches to spirituality; each answered the questions of God, man, and church on the basis of their own understanding of authority; and each lived out their own expression of worship as a result.

Catholic spirituality could be considered as the more progressive faction of the time. The Roman Catholic Church could point back through apostolic succession to the Apostle Peter as the first pope of Rome. Thus, it was "the" institution of worship in western society, and as such sought to maintain its position as final arbiter between man and God regarding all things spiritual; tradition, the ongoing life and practice of the church, was viewed as being equally authoritative as scripture. Both were deemed to be sources of revelation from God: scripture being the original record of the words and works of God given to mankind; tradition being the progressive ongoing revelation given through the church, as history continued to unfold. While tradition and scripture ideally would never contradict, in practice one or the other would have to take precedent as final authority in the life of the church. Catholic spirituality of the medieval era chose tradition.

The Catholic spirituality of the time may be best thought of as an outside to inside approach to relationship with God. Worship consisted of the external actions and practices of going to mass, confession, penance, giving of alms, etc. In the more advanced monastic forms, praying the daily office, vows of poverty, chastity, and obedience, along with surrender of personal choices in favor of communal life, amplified the understanding that a man's spirit within was conditioned to be closer to God through discipline from without. The external actions and disciplines comprised the spiritual life. Through them the interior of the human heart and spirit were conditioned and transformed, outside to inside.

Protestants were the de facto conservatives of the day, reaching back to the roots of Christianity in the Greek New Testament and Apostolic teaching. They sought to correct the church and society from a tradition which they viewed as having erred from God's original revelation in Holy Scripture. *Sola Scriptura*, scripture alone, was the rallying cry of the protestant reformation. Scripture alone was to be the final authority in all matters regarding both spirituality and church. In order for the church to maintain a proper course down through history tradition must yield to scripture, and wherever necessary be corrected by scripture. Naturally, this did not go over well with those who held the reigns of power in the Roman church.

The proponents of protestant spirituality took the opposite approach to their catholic counterparts. Instead of transforming the human spirit within by means of external actions, it was only God's grace, and faith in him alone, that could redeem and transform the inner man. *Sola Fide*, faith alone, and *Sola Gratia*, grace alone, were added to form a triumvirate of theological belief. At best, external actions may only offer evidence of a preceding internal transformation. Works were dead. Worship began with personal prayers and meditation upon God's word, along with an interior knowledge and experience of God's amazing forgiveness and grace. Only afterward were found the external expressions of corporate worship and service to God as evidence of a life transformed, inside to outside.

The dichotomy between catholic and protestant spirituality in many ways continues even to this day. When the Anglican

Church came into being, it was able to draw from each spiritual gene pool, to produce a kind of hybrid vigor. In much of the Anglican expression that follows, this external/internal tension between these spiritualities becomes part of a balanced whole.

In all fairness, both approaches to spirituality were contained within the Roman Catholic Church. Although both were nurtured down through time, the protestant impulse generally found less favor with those in higher authority, as it was seen as a threat to the status quo. Following the protestant reformation there came a Catholic counter reformation, which did indeed address many of the issues which fueled the protestant fires. But, in the sixteenth century these two visions of being Christian came to a flashpoint over the sale of indulgences by the pope in Rome. Luther lit the fire of protest, and the rest as they say is history.

The ensuing conflict engulfed all of Western Europe, with political, social, and ecclesiastic upheaval and realignment. At the time, reformation meant bloodshed, as church and government, armies and populace fought out the passions of their beliefs. In time this fervor spread to England, and the Anglican reformation was under way. Using the occasion of Henry the VIII's marriage predicament, Thomas Cranmer[1] and the English reformers effected a split with Rome and brought about the establishment of the Anglican Church.

Cranmer was influenced by the continental reformers, and especially the Lutheran expression, which had been embraced by his wife. He longed to see a revitalized Christian faith in England, and a restoration of worship throughout the churches of the land. Cranmer's genius lay in his crafting of the Anglican *Book of Common Prayer*, as a means to bring order and conformity to every church in England. In this manner, he reunified the community of faithful on a national scale, for all were to be engaged in same services of prayer on Sundays and throughout the week. In addition, Cranmer instituted the placing and reading of the Holy Scriptures in English in every parish, so that all could hear the word of God in their own language.

1. Appendix II, *Anglican-ism Terms and Characters*

Anglican Re-Formation

Henry VIII, who is commonly known as the founder of the Church of England, was unable to move forward with his own selfish desires for divorce and remarriage, because, as a Roman Catholic, he was subject to the authority of the pope. However, as the reformation proceeded new jurisdictions were being formed based along ethnic and geographical lines, such as the Lutherans in Germany and the Reformed in Geneva. The monarchs, or rulers, of these jurisdictions were deemed to be the heads of the churches in their respective areas.

Cranmer and the other reformers approached Henry with a history lesson: before the Roman Catholic Church came to England and was established under the pope, there was already a Christian church present—the church of St. Patrick. Celtic Christianity had flourished first in Ireland and then throughout most of England from 432 to 597, until Rome sent St. Augustine to establish a Roman Catholic Church at Canterbury. As the Celtic Church and the Roman Church collided, the question needed to be addressed, "Which expression would be valid?" In 664 at the Synod of Whitby, King Oswy, ruled in favor of Rome, and the Celtic Church faded from the scene. Therefore, Cranmer argued that as king, Henry VIII was actually the head of the church in England that existed before Rome ever arrived, and as such could reverse the earlier ruling and grant himself a divorce. Henry got what he wanted, a new marriage and chance for a male heir, but Cranmer and the others who desired reformation in England also achieved their goals, and the Anglican Church came into being.

However, the conflict between protestant and catholic spiritualities, along with the resulting bloodshed, continued unabated until the populace was weary of religious strife. Finally, under the rule of Queen Elizabeth came the Anglican solution: The Via Media.

The Via Media

After years of bloody conflict between catholic and protestant forces in England, Elizabeth came to the throne. In a brilliant stroke of leadership, she gathered and reunified the English people around a new vision for the church and for the nation. Rather than being strictly catholic or strictly protestant, England would choose to compromise between them both: the Via Media, which literally means "middle way." Thus, the first Anglican reformation was stabilized by maintaining that the church would retain the catholic forms of worship—orders, liturgy and sacraments, symbols and vestments—while embracing the protestant reforms of doctrine—sola scriptura, sola fide, sola gratis. The aptly named "Elizabethan Settlement" produced a beautifully harmonized English church, with a unity based in common prayer. Thereby, Anglicans maintained continuity with the catholic tradition of the church, and embraced the protestant return to the roots of Christianity and the authority of Holy Scripture. There remained, however, many who were deeply committed to one side or the other.

It should be added in fairness to the historical record that Elizabeth herself was not so deeply committed to the vision of a church balanced between catholic and protestant ideals. As sovereign of the Church of England, she was decidedly more protestant in her views, especially since being so afforded her greater autonomy to rule according to her own will. The Via Media was a decidedly political solution for her as well as a theological one. Regardless of her intent, a de facto balance resulted from the continuation of sacramental, catholic worship by the masses and the influx of protestant ideals championed by the elite.

Catholic------------Church of England------------Protestant
(Via Media)

More than just a historical event, or a onetime decision, the Via Media, in and of itself, became a kind of doctrine to the Anglican Church. This principle of the middle way, and the willingness to allow for a central spectrum of beliefs and understanding, was a means by which ecclesiastical and doctrinal conflicts could be minimized and church unity strengthened. After the bloodshed of the reformation period, Anglicans welcomed an approach to church life that allowed room for disagreement on the mysteries of the sacraments, while emphasizing the life of the community joined together in common prayer. Indeed, the *Book of Common Prayer* with its recollection of the catholic mass, protestant emphasis on scripture, and unifying quality of ecclesial practice may well be considered the icon of the Via Media down through history unto the present time. "*Lex orandi, lex credenda, lex vivendi,*" the law of praying is the law of believing; the law of believing is the law of living; a beautifully spiritual ideal that unites men and women of faith in a community of prayer, while giving grace for various doctrinal nuances.

The Via Media makes room for differences, gives place for discussion, and allows for agreement to disagree if needed without the breaking of fellowship. This principle works fine when the church and the surrounding culture are immersed in the Christian worldview, when the two visions at either end of the spectrum are catholic Christian and protestant Christian. However, as we shall see, such an approach leaves the Anglican-Ism vulnerable to radical change from an influx of non-Christian beliefs, especially when the principle of the middle way is applied to situations which include theologies and practices that are in conflict with those which are distinctly Christian.

In practice, the Via Media provided a stable vessel which sailed down through history and around the world, tacking sometimes port, to the catholic side, sometimes starboard, to the protestant side, while generally avoiding shipwreck on the reefs beyond the fringe. That is until the present day. This resiliency was due in no small part to the careful work in the beginning when the ship was built. As we continue, let us consider the work of the master craftsmen who laid the keel and set the sails.

The Early Apologists

The Anglican Church faced early challenges to its' legitimacy, as well as the need for theological clarity in explaining this new expression of Christian faith and practice. The question still remained as to how to establish the legitimacy of the Church of England that would counter the claims of heresy, railed against it by Rome. These challenges and needs were addressed by two early apologists: John Jewel and Richard Hooker. Both sought to set the Anglican Church on a sure and certain course to navigate by.

John Jewel

In 1562 John Jewel's *Apology for the Church of England*[2] was published, solidifying Queen Elizabeth's protestant inclinations. Previously, Elizabeth had played her intentions close to the vest. Many of the populace hoped for, and saw signs, that she may return the English church to full communion with Rome. However, protestant ideals and national pride had taken root in the English people, as well as their queen, and the schism with Rome was not to be rectified. Jewel's *Apology* takes up the task of legitimizing the Church of England from both a theological and ecclesiological standpoint. In doing so he supersedes and condemns the Church of Rome as apostate, and instead grounds the Church of England on the apostles, the primitive church, and the early fathers. What follows then is a summary of the main points of his argument.

Jewel's opening salvos in section one of the *Apology* refutes the charge of heresy. He portrays the Church of England as the faithful servant of God's truth, whom as a result is persecuted. Thus, he aligns the Church of England with Christ, Paul, and Stephen in the New Testament, and Isaiah, Jeremiah and Daniel in the Old Testament. As they were persecuted, so also those who profess the Gospel in England are also being persecuted. Having established solidarity with the prophets, apostles, and martyrs of scripture, as well as Jesus Christ, Jewel further refutes the charges of heresy by insisting on a return to the doctrine of the fathers and primitive church. Finally, he asserts Holy Scripture as the final judge and arbiter of heresy, wresting away authority from the pope in matters of doctrine.

2. Jewel, John. *An Apology of the Church of England*

Thus, Jewel nullifies the preeminence of the pope, while retaining the conciliar bishopric of the early church. A move that is distinctly different from other reformers. This is a position that we will return to in advocating re-formation now in the twenty-first century. The protestant nature of Jewel's argument is further elucidated by several doctrinal positions. Marriage is sanctioned as holy for all persons, including priests. Two sacraments are affirmed: baptism and Eucharist. Communion is to be given in both kinds. Both the bread and the wine were to be administered to the people. Also the doctrine of transubstantiation is expressly denied. Roman theology continued to hold that the bread and wine literally became the flesh and blood of Christ through a change in their substance.

Justification by faith, services said in English, and Christ as the only mediator complete Jewel's creed of Christian belief and closely align the Church of England with the continental reformers. In the heart of his *Apology*, Jewel lambastes the pope and Rome on the right, and severs all connection with fringe groups on the left. He compares the radical reformers, i.e. the Anabaptists, to previous heretical groups such as the Arians, Marcionites, etc. On the other hand, the pope and his legates, along with the immoral practices and schemes for money, are all the subject of biting invective.

In reflection, Jewel's *Apology for the Church of England* is very thorough and convincing. He idealizes the English church as the pure, authentic expression of Christianity, artfully weaving connections with the apostles, the fathers, and the primitive church. The Church of England is true Christianity which has shaken itself free from the corruption of Rome. He turns the charge of heresy back on the accusers, redefines authority to exclude preeminence by the pope, and exalts the power and position of the Monarch. Throughout, he establishes a decidedly protestant charter for the Church of England, and vindicates Queen Elizabeth as its head.

Richard Hooker

Whereas Jewel sought to vindicate the Church of England from the charges of heresy, and to establish it as a faithful continuation of the early church, Richard Hooker took a step further in defining Anglican theological belief. Hooker is an important father of the Anglican-Ism, one who is often quoted in support of the various theological positions today. Yet, one that is also often misunderstood when attempting to apply his thought to our current historical context. In particular, his promotion of three authoritative sources for Christian belief and practice: scripture, tradition, and reason.

Richard Hooker lived at the time of the reformation, and was thoroughly immersed in the late medieval worldview. In his time the world was understood in a hierarchical fashion. God was a God of order, who fashioned creation and society in such a manner that it displayed that order. Each person had their place in society, and the grace of God trickled down through his anointed monarchs and the church unto the rest of the people.

Thus, we find in Hooker a holistic system of authority, which resonated from the top down, beginning with God and flowing through his appointed channels and social institutions. Individual identity and authority was drawn from a person's place in the whole. Authority resided in God and is expressed by the scripture. Tradition provided and ongoing reservoir for the results of that expression, and reason was the means by which we engage with both in the present. Thus, reason had its place within the hierarchy, rather than standing apart from it in judgment.

Over time Hooker's three categories have developed into a kind of symbol, of Anglican belief known as "the three-legged stool." Each of the legs being viewed as having equal authority. While this may be an elegant concept, it is in fact antithetical to Hooker's original thought, and the time in which he live.

The concept of the three-legged stool as a model for authority in the Anglican Church developed later, as a consequence of three primary strands of ecclesial expression gaining prominence in the time period after the Enlightenment: the evangelicals, the anglo-catholics and the liberals. These three parties coexisting in one church allowed a superficial illusion to emerge that espoused three different sources of truth as their basis, namely scripture, tradition and reason. This led to the image of the three legs of a stool, each source being equal to the other. The evangelicals favored scripture, the anglo-catholics looked to tradition, and the liberals espoused reason as primacy.[3]

Scripture, tradition, and reason are not three wells which individual Anglicans draw from at will to support their own autonomous authority. They are not some mythological stool upon which Anglicanism sits. Hooker in particular did not believe this. The interface of scripture, tradition and reason is much more complicated. The God given faculty of reason enables us to make sense out of the creation around us, and to partake of divine revelation via the scripture. The scripture informs tradition, the ongoing life of the community of believers, and the community interprets scripture in the present. Ultimately authority resides in God himself. His authority is manifested by means of the Holy Spirit through the scripture and the community. Reason may be thought of as that combination of faculties which enable us to encounter and know God, but never as an independent judge over the truth of His revelation.

Anglican Comprehensiveness

Jewel and Hooker maintained and expanded the Anglican-Ism, widening the walls to allow for catholic form and offices, while maintaining protestant ideals of scripture and faith. In the process, the way was made to incorporate the prevailing understanding of reason and authority, thus strengthening and expanding the Via Media even further. In Hooker we see the beginning of the interaction of the church with the ideals of the surrounding culture. The Enlightenment period upheld reason as the highest value,

---

3. Fairfield, Les. *Lecture on Richard Hooker*

and Hooker brought reason into the matrix of the middle way, in order to balance it with scripture and tradition. Thus, we see an acknowledgement of the values of modernity, which then becomes an ongoing practice as history unfolds—the importation of values and ideas from the surrounding culture into the matrix of the Via Media.

The stage was set, the foundation laid, comprehensiveness was now in the DNA of Anglicanism. A principle was established that allowed for a spectrum of belief. Catholic and protestant poles had been established and affirmed, and now the challenge to find the balance was to begin. As we move down through the history that follows, the pendulum begins to swing back and forth from one side to the other, with each swing bringing more into the mix. Let us consider two important movements which continue to exert influence to this day: The Evangelical Revival and The Oxford Movement.

In mode of operation the Via Media spread out its branches over both the catholic and protestant ideals, seeking to gather as much as possible into the center. This resulted in a comprehensiveness that made room for subtle differences of belief, along with more contradictory assertions of faith. Anglican comprehensiveness reflects that proper polite, and somewhat stoic, model of English sensibility. No one wanted to return to the religious conflicts of the past, so, for heaven's sake, let's agree to disagree and maintain unity through common worship with the *Book of Common Prayer*.

The principle of this comprehensive unity has continued even to this day. At times, it has allowed for marvelous interactions and synthesis of Christian thought. Especially since those with new understandings were not burned alive as heretics. However, at other times Anglican comprehensiveness alone was insufficient to contain, or retain, movements that pulled out in new directions-movements such as the Evangelical Revival, led by the Wesleys and George Whitefield. Evangelicals today may be surprised to learn they started out as Anglicans.

In the 1800s the pendulum swung back to the catholic side of the Via Media with the advent of the Oxford Movement, which celebrated the more catholic forms of worship. The Oxford fellows embraced a high view of the Church of England which had been advocated by William Laud and the Arminians. They looked to the primitive apostolic church as the ideal, and sought strict obedience to church tradition. Indeed, the tradition of the church was affirmed as an equal authority with scripture, the two strands running parallel with one another down through history. Thus, the historic episcopate retained authority in all matters of church polity, and should in no way be superseded by the secular authority of parliament.

Of course, these high church proclivities opened the Oxford Movement to Puritan criticism, and charges of popery, as it had done to their predecessors. While the Oxford Movement embraced the high expression of church life in many ways it differed subtly by drawing in elements and attitudes found in other quarters. Along with structured, "high", community life, the Oxford fellows desired an experience of God and personal piety that was reflective of the Evangelicals. Theirs was a worship of the heart not just the head.

The acceptance and incorporation of the expressions embodied by the Oxford Movement and Evangelical Revival, further expanded and strengthened the principal of Anglican comprehensiveness. As a result, the way was made for yet new arrivals of thought and practice to also come in to the Anglican fold, as they emerged from their current historical paradigms.

In response to the attacks of higher criticism in the modern period, a liberal protestant expression emerged. Liberal Protestantism split out from the evangelicals taking with them the focus on social activism as the heart of the gospel. The emphasis on conversion experience became simply spiritual experience, and biblicism was set aside in the light of modern reason. So, Anglicanism now had three poles of Christian expression within: catholic, evangelical, and liberal.

As history flows a bit further into the twentieth century, the charismatic revivals began to take place. Taking spiritual experience in a different direction, the main emphasis was now on the power and gifts of the Holy Spirit within the church in our time. At first this movement was contained within the existing vessels of church expression, but soon moved out to become a pole in and of itself. Thus, as we come down through time to the present we find catholic and protestant further developed into catholic, evangelical, liberal, and charismatic. All of them accepted within the Anglican fold, due to the principle of comprehensiveness which we found from the beginning.

The danger with this quiet comprehensive approach to Christian faith and practice is that eventually it can simply become an excuse to allow anyone to believe anything that seems proper to themselves. Like a man who eats whatever he likes, whenever he wants, eventually he will end up unable to move. Comprehensiveness leads to inertia. In order to get back to life he must have some discipline and exercise. In like manner in order to be healthy and energetic, Anglican comprehensiveness must engage in the more difficult task of going on a diet from time to time.

Autonomous Fellowship and the Chicago-Lambeth Quadrilateral

The Anglican Church grew and the Anglican-Ism expanded, exponentially along with the British Empire. Colonialism meant that Anglican churches were planted in countries around the world. Province by province the Church of England was transformed into a church of the world—the Anglican Communion. Provinces were set up that essentially mirrored the polity of the original, with bishops and archbishops in authority. What emerged from this process is another guiding principle of Anglican-Ism known as autonomous fellowship.

Each province of the Anglican Church was deemed to be autonomous. That is to say that there was no central adjudicating authority, such as the Roman Catholic pope, or even perhaps a metropolitan of the Orthodox Church. While individual differences did develop within the various polities of the provinces, all adhered to the autonomous rule of the bishops, who were duly consecrated in turn from those who preceded them. This allowed for the ability to flex and adjust to local context. It has been said that this principle of autonomy was the genius of the Anglican-Ism. More recently it has been said the same lack of a central authority has proved to be the Anglican-Ism's Achilles heel.

Autonomous fellowship developed as a desire for the sharing of church life across the nations in a way that was non-coercive, and in a manner that did not give power to the powerful. That is to say, this allowed for the Anglican churches that were planted during colonialism, to become un-colonial by being able to provide oversight for themselves.

The principle of autonomy did not necessarily promote the independence of each province to do as they pleased; instead, it affirmed the interdependence of each province, as equals with one another. Once again, we must remember that, by and large, there was widespread agreement of Christian belief and practice. *The Book of Common Prayer*, the Via Media, and in general a Christian worldview were prevalent throughout the eighteenth and nineteenth centuries, until Christendom began grappling with the paradigm shift of modernity. Nevertheless, as we approach the twentieth century, the question began to be raised, "What is Anglican-Ism?" "How will we define who or what we are?" "What is the nature of the relationship between professing Anglican churches?" Novel concepts it would seem, because for the most part the whole ethos, the Anglican-Ism, was just taken for granted.

In order to answer the questions of relationship, communion, and commonality, Anglican bishops from around the world came together in council and discussion, first in Chicago in 1886, then two years later at Lambeth, England in 1888. The result was the production of the four basic tenets that defined the Anglican Communion. The Chicago-Lambeth Quadrilateral declares this is what defines us as Anglicans, that to which all agree upon and binds our common life together:

1. The Holy Scriptures of the Old and New Testament as the revealed Word of God.
2. The Nicene Creed as the sufficient statement of the Christian Faith.

3. The two Sacraments,-Baptism and the Supper of the Lord,—ministered with the unfailing use of Christ's words of institution and of the elements ordained by Him.

4. The Historic Episcopate, locally adapted in the methods of its administration to the varying needs of the nations and peoples called of God into the unity of His Church.[4]

Thus, autonomous fellowship remained as the order of the day, along with a fresh articulation of the four cornerstones upon which rested the Anglican Cathedral. This fourfold description of Anglican belief and practice remains definitive unto this day, and was sufficient to handle the challenges of the modern era. The problem being that, now, we are no longer living in the modern era, as we shall discuss in the next chapter on paradigms.

The Big Tent

The twentieth century witnessed the expansion of the theological/ecclesial spectrum within the Anglican-Ism in several significant ways. As mentioned previously, the polarity between catholic and protestant, morphed into a grid with four distinct expressions: catholic, evangelical, charismatic, and liberal. Each of these had their own particular theological emphasis, spirituality, and agenda. Thus, the two poles of Anglican-Ism became four, all set within the borders of the Anglican Communion. Yet, all continued to touch upon the broader developing historical streams of Christianity in general. The Anglican Church became a big tent, where it would seem everyone was welcome. A place where differences were set aside and all could be together regardless of particular theologies and practices.

Fast forwarding to the present, then, what we find in operation as a principle of common life is the concept of the big tent. All are welcome to come in, the doors open outward, and inward, in all directions. Inside the big tent there is a lot of activity. We find not just the typical three ring circus, but four: Four centers of

4. Appendix I, *Chicago-Lambeth Quadrilateral*

spirituality; four centers of theology; four grandstands gathering four communities around centers of activity and purpose. The big tent represents the culmination of the comprehensiveness inherent in the Church of England from the beginning. As noted earlier, this was the genius of the Anglican-Ism, and now, this has also become its downfall.

Within the tent, we find four baptismal fonts filled from the historic streams of Christian expression, but with little connection or accountability between them. Each is steadily baptizing converts into their own respective systems of belief. Within the tent, we find all the excitement, the energy, the pageantry of a four-ring circus, but no ringmaster to coordinate, or oversee the results. The tent itself is held up by the four poles of the Lambeth Quadrilateral, but there are no side panels—no boundaries to the outside world. Thus, the big tent is vulnerable to collapse when the winds blow.

Conclusion

There definitely is an Anglican stream of Christianity flowing from the Reformation of the sixteenth century, a mixture of tributaries that flow from the headwaters of catholic and protestant ecclesiology. Along the way, other tributaries have joined in; evangelical, charismatic, and liberal currents have become well established. And so, the Anglican Church is now multifaceted, with a broad spectrum of theological beliefs and practices. For better or worse, comprehensiveness and the dictum to find the middle way comprise major components of the Anglican expression of Christianity as it flows forward in history.

The principle of openness among the churches of the communion and to the world, is expressed through a sense of autonomy and willingness to adapt to the surrounding cultural context. The benefit of openness has allowed the Anglican-Ism to spread worldwide, bringing the church to a multitude of different languages and peoples. Yet, now this same openness leaves a vulnerability to the reverse as well. Instead of the gospel flowing out to the surrounding culture, the ideologies of the surrounding culture have flowed backwards into the church. Indeed, I would argue that the Anglican Church has no inherent boundaries within itself. Rather, in openness it has allowed the surrounding culture to set the boundaries for it. Hence, when a major paradigm shift occurs, the boundaries are subject to readjustment, or in being discarded altogether.

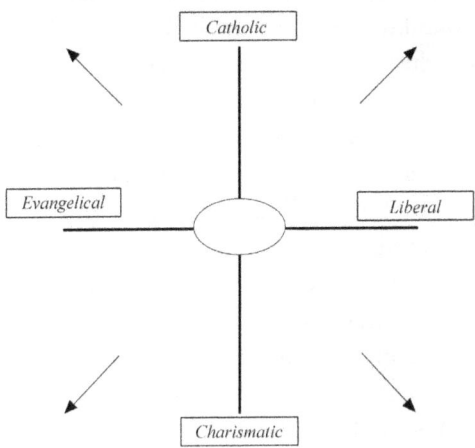

**The four poles of Christian expression incorporated into the Anglican-Ism
Arrows depict the intentional movement or promotion to the surrounding world
Note: There are no boundaries to prevent the reversal of the arrows
Thereby allowing the world to flow into the church**

The graph in figure 1–3 is representative of the Anglican Church today. The four poles of Christian expression are not only indicative of the Anglican-Ism, but are also true of the Christian Church as a whole. Historically, the river of Christianity has split into a variety of streams and rivulets. The process began with the Great Schism of 1054, which divided Eastern Orthodox with Roman Catholic expressions. The Reformation separated the protestant stream from within the western tributary, forming Lutheran, Reformed, Anglican and Anabaptist variations. Subsequently, protestants continued to split from one another, as evangelical, liberal, and charismatic expressions formed and went off on their own way.

Practically speaking these four streams of Christianity, which were all present in the beginning, continue to incorporate the major portions of the worldwide church in our time. This is the community of the church, as practiced by the faithful, and as seen by the world. Indeed, each of the four streams has captured and contained within itself a portion of the Gospel of Jesus Christ, vibrant elements which are part of the whole. Churches have then polarized around their own particular elements of the faith, most often to the exclusion of the others. What all need to realize is that each of the four make up a vital part of the whole. In fact, I will argue that they all need each other to stay in balance. Separated from one another in isolation each and every expression has more potential to go off track—to flow off on a tangent leaving genuine Christianity behind.

The Anglican Church, the church of the Via Media, not surprisingly finds itself flowing in the middle of the streambeds. All four of these major expressions have been accepted as valid within the Anglican-Ism. But, this is not to say they have been all brought together in a balanced whole. Usually individual churches within the Anglican stream embrace and polarize around one or the other of these poles just like the more broadly defined streams of the church as a whole. Nevertheless, the potential for wholeness does reside in the Anglican Church. It is here that all are included, all are able to inform one another, all correct one another, and all contribute to a sum which is greater than the individual parts.

Furthermore, as the church in the middle of it all, Anglicans are uniquely situated in Christendom to bring together the major streams flowing around them. They all share a connection of one expression or another that is already accepted in Anglicanism. Thus, we have a common starting point from which we can relate to one another. We have a mode of fellowship and understanding already in place. Being in the middle means Anglicans can talk to everyone.

Where would you locate your church on the graph?

The Anglican-Ism is comprehensive, it is open, and it has vitality. It has from the beginning been a fervent mix of many of the vibrant expression of Christian faith, which are themselves often polarized and isolated within their own church contexts. Catholic, evangelical, charismatic, and liberal streams, when allowed to inform and balance one another, have great potential to enhance and create a wholeness in worship and community life that is much needed to engage the world in the emerging paradigm of the twenty-first century. On a personal note, this is why I became an Anglican to begin with.

In order to be effective, and, at the same time overcome the vulnerabilities which have led to the current crisis in the Anglican Communion, the Anglican-Ism which has brought us this far needs adjustment. Before moving to a discussion of the immediate problems and solutions, first let us consider the paradigm shifts through which the Anglican-Ism has already come, and the one which is now upon us, in the next chapter—Paradigm to Paradigm.

Paradigm Shift:
"A change in a fundamental model of events"
—THOMAS KUHN

Chapter 2
Paradigm to Paradigm

The term paradigm comes from the philosophy of science and is defined as a "generally accepted model of how ideas relate to one another and form a conceptual framework, which scientific research is then carried out within." Paradigms exist within science, but they are not limited to science. We all have our own personal paradigm—our beliefs, values, activities and routines that enable us to function. Societies function through relationships made possible by mutual assent to the reigning paradigm, those beliefs that are commonly held and known to be right. Although we rarely give thought to its existence, paradigms provide the operating system that allows us to function and to interact with one another. Over time these modes of operation become entrenched in whole eras of history. That is until the next version comes along.

Paradigm to Paradigm

Socio-historical paradigms are just that, a particular ordering of social interactions and understanding within a historical time period. One that provides an operating system that allows the society to function. While this type of paradigm is definitely real, it is mostly invisible. It exists beneath the surface in the assumptions of what is true, and the presuppositions of what is real. It becomes self-perpetuating through a myriad of subtle communications, which we intuitively receive and incorporate into our lives. In this manner we just know what is and is not proper behavior without even consciously thinking about it.

The components of a historical paradigm are scientific, technological, religious, spiritual, and even emotional. Our values, beliefs, morals/ethics, and rituals are embedded in the paradigm that surrounds us. We believe the world is what it is because it feels right. All the complexities of human data and interaction feed into the formation of the reigning paradigm. This is mostly invisible, beneath the conscious awareness within social exchanges, but often readily seen in the artwork of an era, or now, especially in the films and TV ads that provide our reflection in the mirror.

Paradigms reign because they work, at least for a time and in the time of their historical era. The agreed upon elements remain in place until they are cast down by new irrefutable insights, become irrelevant, or simply cease to function because the world has moved on. When the telephone was invented, the telegraph ceased to exist. When cell phones came to be land lines ceased. When they invent the microchip that inserts into the bone above your ear, cell phones will no longer be needed. Paradigm to paradigm. This simple illustration has been played out on a much larger scale throughout history. In ancient times Ptolemy demonstrated that the earth was the center of the universe. Everyone knew it was true. It felt right. It affected the way we understood our humanity. Then came the Renaissance and the Copernican revolution. The previous era in history was overturned, and the sun became the center of the universe. This change set off a chain reaction amongst the other elements throughout the reigning paradigm, testing and trying them for relevance in the new order. A paradigm shift was underway.

The process of shifting from paradigm to paradigm has been a common occurrence in Western history. A certain way of living and being a society gains ascendency and makes sense of the facts and values present in a particular time period. An operating system develops that functions and continues until it begins to decay. At times, new facts emerge, which then unravel the system. Assumptions are proven to be false, or generally accepted principles no longer hold together. The shift begins to a new, revised set of criteria, often accompanied by a period of uncertainty and anxiety until things settle into place once again. A new paradigm emerges.

The new paradigm makes sense to the culture and to the time. Populace, governance, education, and religious institutions all readjust to keep step with the new paradigm. Most importantly, in the collective conscious, or perhaps subconscious, the basic assumptions and presuppositions of the new paradigm become the accepted norms for social interaction. Everyone knows, or comes to understand, and agrees that this is the right way to think and act. The lens of the new paradigm becomes the way in which the world around us is viewed and accepted by everyone. Well, almost everyone.

With every paradigm shift there are always those holdouts, those who remain stuck in the old way of thinking. But, as the river flows onward, time wears them down and pushes them aside into quiet eddies alongside that swirl. They become trapped in their own momentum. These eddies are often viewed as irrelevant and antiquated by the main stream, or at times even threatening or intolerable. They are the ones who simply don't get it and refuse to go along with the program.

All institutions of society must adjust to the new paradigms when they come. The church in particular often faces great challenges, especially when the dogma, worship, and morality promoted by the church are perceived as threats to the new order of the day. This is true when the church, or elements within the church, are viewed as irrelevant, or ineffective, and seen as part of the problems of the past rather than the solutions for the present. In these times the pressure mounts for them to be discarded. The adjustment between church, culture, and the new paradigm is further complicated by virtue of the fact that the church itself is also totally immersed in the surrounding culture, the people who make up the church also live, work, and participate daily in the world. Thus, the members of the church will also be influenced toward the position of the new paradigm, thinking along with the world that it is right and good and that it makes sense.

At times the church may find itself in active participation with the shift. Sometimes the changes made fit hand in hand with the traditional Biblical viewpoint, as in the case of the abolishment of slavery during the paradigm shift of the Enlightenment. Sometimes the changes are more accommodating to the surrounding culture, as in the present-day case of same sex marriage. Due to the conservative nature of the church throughout most of Western history we more often find ourselves on the defense, at odds with society or at least with key principles of each succeeding paradigm shift. This, I believe, is one of the essential calls of the Christian Church, to be a prophetic witness to all generations.

For our purposes, it is important to note how much the church is a participant of the reigning paradigm in contrast with how much it stands apart, either in isolation or prophetic witness. Paradigm to paradigm what are some of the key changes that have taken place in society, and how have they elicited change in turn from the church? The challenge to the church in general is to continue to faithfully preach the Gospel, the faith once delivered to the saints, within the context of the historical paradigm in which we live. The holy mystery of the church, which is the body of Christ, is designed to present to every age the certainty of salvation through Jesus Christ, in a manner that is relevant, yet, at the same time uncompromising—a sacramental witness that speaks directly to the hearts, minds, and souls of the world around us.

The strength of the Anglican Church has been its flexibility in adapting to the paradigm shifts of Western civilization. The elements that constitute the Anglican-Ism form a broad spectrum of contact points between Christian faith and the secular world, which when functioning properly allow the Gospel to flow outward into society at large. The weakness of the Anglican Church is that when proper boundaries are not maintained the flow is reversed, and the secular world flows into the church. The Anglican-Ism then becomes an extension of the Human-Ism.

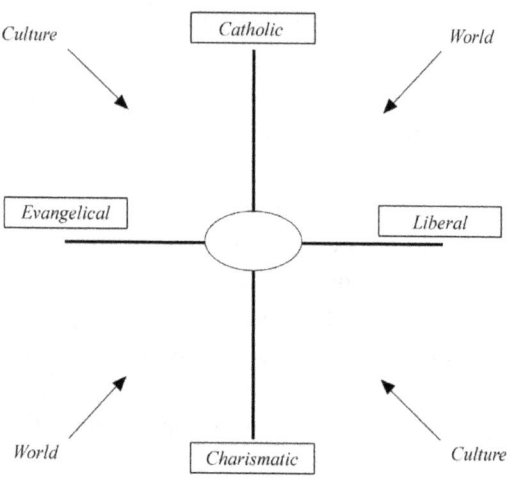

**The four poles of Christian expression incorporated into the Anglican-Ism
Arrows depict the intentional movement in from the surrounding world**

If we were to make an analysis of historical paradigm shifts all the way back to ancient times, we would observe an ever-increasing closeness of cultures, economies, and religions, along with an ever decreasing constriction of time in between each shift. Because we are concerned with an Anglican perspective, we will engage the process from the time of the reformation, and the paradigm in which the Church of England came into being. Let us take a brief survey through the major paradigm shifts, considering the social contexts, prevailing values, and some of the ways the Anglican Church adapted in each era.

Paradigm to Paradigm

Paradigm	Social Context	Values	Adaptation
Premodern	Western Christian	Tradition	Catholic
Modern	Enlightenment	Reason	Via Media
Postmodern	Pluralism	Experience	Spirituality
One-world*	Unified	Participation	Community

*So named by the author to describe the next paradigm shift which is currently unfolding

The Premodern Paradigm

In the premodern era, Christians espoused a sacramental worldview in which the spiritual realm infused the material realm with meaning, purpose, and danger. By means of ritual a person intertwined his/her life with the grace of God flowing through the sacraments. As the devil strove for dominion over the souls of men and women, liturgy and sacrament brought the assurance of escape from the clutches of evil. The rhythm of worship enhanced by incense, bells, and all sorts of tactile actions yielded a holistic spirituality that engaged all the senses. Unfortunately, this same sacramental expression often broke out of the bounds of Christianity resulting in charms and incantations to ward off evil, and the veneration of shrines and relics.

In the West, this mode of worship culminated in Medieval society organized around the ideal of Christendom at large. All of Western Europe and the British Isles considered themselves inheritors of the Christian faith, organized around the original concept of the Holy Roman Empire. During this time society was ordered by a divinely appointed hierarchy:

> God
> Kings and Pope
> Lord's and Bishops
> Merchants and Priests
> Peasants

Non-Christians

This was seen as the natural order, appointed by God himself. One did not question their place in society, nor the authority of church and king. The earth was the center of the universe, and mankind God's special purpose on it.

In the late medieval period, popular Christianity found expression in a variety of ways which have persisted in the Church of England even unto the present. In contrast to the word based faith of the Reformation, medieval piety celebrated the life of faith through pictures and stories, ritual and sacrament. The appeal of this kind of spirituality should not be oversimplified, by relegating it to ignorance, or lack of education. Rather, the tenacity of medieval expressions of faith and worship points toward something deeper—an inclination within the being of mankind to worship and encounter God by means of symbols.

This symbolic expression of late medieval piety has persisted down through history because it is closely aligned with a Biblical worldview, and offers a holistic form of worship. It resonates with a part of our being often denied in modernity, but now is once again being reaffirmed in the postmodern period. Today the beauty of holiness embraced by the pre-modern church again speaks to the heart of postmodern men and women. Yet, to avoid the errors and excesses inherent to this right brained, experiential, expression of faith, we must provide the rudder of modern propositional understanding. The two are not mutually exclusive, but balance and enhance one another into a genuine, authentic, and whole manifestation of Christian Faith.

It is important to remember that the Anglican Church was birthed in the premodern era. Christendom remained the order of the day in Western European society. To be sure, the Reformation itself was giving place to a critical evaluation of doctrines and polities, resulting in the breakup of the monolithic Roman Catholic Church. However, the reigning paradigm of the social order remained intact. The society that surrounded the Anglican Church was Christian—traditional Christian: one that upheld the authority of Holy Scripture; the authority of the church; and the authority of the monarchy. The prevailing ethics and values, the accepted norms of social discourse, were grounded in a biblical worldview—what we would call today the Judeo-Christian foundation of Western society. The Church of England had to find its way through the catholic vs. protestant dilemma, but it did so in a solidly Christian faith based context.

In the 1500s many of the elements which comprised the foundation of the premodern paradigm began to break down. The traditional authorities of church and king began to come into question. The long-accepted hierarchy of society gave way to rising classes of merchants and craftsmen. Instead of a Christendom there came the formation of nation states, unified in common language and commercial interests. Western culture was weary with the wars of religion, and longed for a new basis for human interaction and morality. Amazing breakthroughs began to take place in science and exploration, and the age of discovery was upon us. It was the age of enlightenment and reason was the light.

The Modern Paradigm

With the advent of the Enlightenment period, the social order moved forward with the paradigm shift to Modernity. Science and reason became the new authorities of the day. Nothing was beyond the razor of mankind's scintillating intellect—our critical rational power. Especially suspect were those authorities which were an integral part of the previous system of thought. The authority of tradition, the Bible, and the church were now deemed at best irrelevant, or at worst in opposition to the new order. Thus, scientific method and higher criticism were wielded as weapons designed to tear apart any perceived threat from the previous paradigm.

The achievement and honor of the individual became highly prized and valued. This was to be an age of exploration and discovery by explorers and scientists alike, with a concept of social evolution destining the exceptional for the top of society. It did not matter on which level you were born, upward mobility awaited any that could attain it. Rapid advances in technology, medicine, and understanding of the natural world resulted in an optimism which concluded that mankind could solve any and all problems given enough time and energy. In the Medieval time stability and order were valued, keeping on with the way things had been. Modernity embraced change for change sake. Change itself became a principle of operation. Rationalism—empiricism—individualism—optimism these are the foundational values upon which the modern era was constructed.

PREMODERN	MODERN	POSTMODERN

"Because God put it there and that's the way it's always been."	"Onwards and upwards with inevitable progress!"	"Bllpppggghljsdlkfjowejfalsk djflksdjflksjdldjl;aldflkj;;;;df"

Throughout the modern era, theologians and churchmen grappled with the assault from the new secular thinking, and the new secular institutions, which challenged the veracity of scripture and denigrated faith into a fairytale and superstition. Seeking continued relevancy, the protestant churches in particular espoused a revised "liberal theology", which presented faith as grounded in the subjective experience of the believer. Religion was reconstituted as a social construct, one necessary for the good of humanity, reigning in the negative excesses of the desires of the individual self. In the modern era faith became an experience and religion a movement. Both were set aside from discourse in the public arena and relegated to the private sphere. It is at this time that the fracture began in the Anglican Church and by extension in Christianity at large.

While the older, traditional views continued to spread into the new Anglican churches which were growing around the world, in Africa, Asia, and South America, in the West a new liberal vision came into being. As we shall see, this liberal expression took as its starting point a very different set of presuppositions and practices than those found in the traditional biblical worldview. A new foundation for belief in God was laid by German theologians like Schliermacher and Hegel. Their innovation was to claim subjective experience with God as holy ground, unassailable by the tenets of modernity. This vision continued to grow and develop down through the modern era of the twentieth century, with a deepening of the sense of the self as authoritative in experience with the divine. This was fused with a theological commitment to an amplified understanding of divine immanence, promoted by popular theologians like Paul Tillich. The result was an experientially oriented theological grid, which was open to direction from the surrounding culture-a ready vessel to embrace the postmodern paradigm shift.

Meanwhile the world was shrinking.

The Postmodern Paradigm

As we near the end of the twentieth century, the tenets of the modern paradigm—individualism, rationalism, optimism, and innovation—have lost their veracity in providing answers to surrounding culture. Their ability to cope with the conditions and conflicts foisted upon humanity was compromised and bogged down, as countries, cultures, languages, and religions have come crashing together.

Historians and scholars recognize that another paradigm shift has taken place. We have left the modern age and entered into what is called the postmodern era. This new era is characterized by radical religious and ideological pluralism, an information explosion, the relativity of truth, and the creation of individual realities. The net result of these phenomena is a seething social cauldron which periodically boils over with alarming results.

Anglican Re-Formation

Pluralism, defined as various religious, cultural, and ideological expressions, has always been present, de facto, in the world. Throughout human history vast empires and cultures have developed dramatically different worldviews. However, until recently these worldviews have been practically isolated from one another by virtue of the sheer distances that separated them. Now in the postmodern paradigm, pluralism has become a prevailing value, especially in regards to religious life. All religions are valued as equal, normative paths to experience the divine.

In our abandonment of objective truth, we now find ourselves in a world of competing relative truths. Anyone can establish anything as a truth claim and thereby gain power in correlation to their ability to persuade others of the validity of that claim. Truth is what you can persuade others to believe. Although most systems of truth have roots in various religious expressions from the modern, premodern, or even ancient ages, there is no idiom within society to prevent the invention of, or synthesizing of new religious movements. This process is known as syncretism, and continues to be very active and popular in our time.

As a counterbalance to the power struggle that comes as a natural outgrowth of pluralism, the postmodern era has embraced tolerance as another preeminent value. Tolerance attempts to disconnect competing systems of belief from striving with one another. Let's take the fighters out of the ring, and all sit down and have a cup of tea together. Your way is right for you. My way is right for me. It is not necessary for us to convince one another, or try to undermine one another. Instead, let us be tolerant, disengaged from the fight and all will be well. The promotion of tolerance as a vital part of post-modern morality cannot be understated. How else can we save ourselves from the wars of religion that are coming in the twenty-first century? The problem of course is that tolerance very quickly becomes intolerance when anyone attempts a truth claim that is construed as universal. "Marriage is designed by God to be between one man and one woman." Run for your life! This kind of thought will not be tolerated. Tolerance then becomes yet another means of persuasion, used to disarm the competition until my view can prevail. Remember postmodern truth is what you can persuade others to believe. Nowhere can this be seen more clearly than in the workings of the Anglican Communion as a whole. Again, Anglicanism seems to find itself in the middle of it all.

Pluralism has leapt out of history to become a defining value of the postmodern age. Relativism and tolerance join in the new value system, promising liberation and squelching opposition. The rapid transference of ideas, money, and people made possible by the advance of technology promise quantitative and qualitative increase in the intensity of pluralistic exchange. Societies, and indeed, civilization itself, hang in the balance as they grapple with emerging problems, conflicts, and partial solutions. Yet, even as we have begun to come to terms with the dynamics of what has come to be known as postmodernity, another historical paradigm shift has already begun to take place beneath our feet.

The One-world Era

Turning into the twentieth century, postmodernity itself is beginning to show signs of disintegration, as a new paradigm is emerging. For my purposes, I have named this new time period The One-world Era. I think most would agree this is exactly what we are dealing with. This next paradigm shift is under way even as I write. The salad buffet of the postmodern era is being put into the blender, turned into cream of vegetable soup, and served hot and steaming to a world that is bound together as one. As we conclude this reflection on the Anglican Church in relation to the historical paradigms shifts in the West, let us now consider the signs and evidence of the new one-world paradigm which is in formation all around us.

The evidence for a shift out of the postmodern era into a new paradigm is mounting. This new one-world era is seen first in the economic realities and challenges which are now taking place in the world. Countries no longer have independent control over their own economies. All nations are already linked together in a de facto one-world economy. When the United States economy goes into recession, it affects Europe, which in turn affects the third world. China, India, Brazil, and Russia are up and coming economic powerhouses, but the interdependence of them all with the rest of the world cannot be denied: "When a butterfly flaps its wings in Beijing, it rains in Detroit;" "When the United States sneezes, the world catches cold." Thus, the very dynamics of the time we live in are putting pressure on all to bring productivity, labor, trade, and currency into some kind of unified system. The systems currently running in old paradigm mode will at some point be unable to keep the pace, resulting in crisis, creative destruction, and replacement with the new.

Not only is the world ever increasingly linked together economically, but in several other ways as well. Ecologically we are all sharing the same finite planet. Concerns for global warming, pollution controls, over fishing international waters, genetic engineering of the food supply, and the green movement in general show one-world thinking and actions that are increasingly taking center stage. Communication is now instant around the globe. That means that the sharing of ideas, attitudes, and relationships is also now instant. Humanity is connected. Humanity is in relationship with itself. No matter where you may happen to find yourself on the planet no longer are you separate from the whole.

The concept of being a citizen of the world is emerging and gaining strength and credibility. Think globally act locally.

So, what remains to complete a one-world paradigm? First, we have yet to witness a political solution that transcends the nation states, bringing all into a worldwide government. This may not be as farfetched, nor as far away at one may think. Historically, governments and empires come and go; to believe that we are somehow immune from this process is somewhat naïve. Also required for the new one-world era, and of special importance to us as Christians, is the emergence of a one-world religion. As the radicalization of the tenets of modernity resulted in the paradigm shift to the postmodern era, so to the radicalization of tenets of postmodernity pluralism will result in a fusion into one religious system: pluralism dictates that all religions be treated as valid and equal, the logical conclusion is a unified religion which synchronizes all into a harmony of faith; monism provides the new theological ideal of religions all worshipping the same divine force according to their cultural formation; relativism and tolerance will call for the celebration of all, not as distinct from one another, but as a multifaceted jewel—all parts of the whole; finally, the fear of religious conflicts and wars, and perhaps radical Islam, will drive even the desire of atheists to find an amenable solution.

The principle of a one-world religion is already the desire of many, and the syncretism needed to produce such a faith is at work in the spirit of the age that surrounds us. The liberal vision of The Episcopal Church and other mainstream protestant churches, combined with a similar impetus in the various religions, could soon produce such a one-world religion. One need simply review the work of the United Religions Initiative sponsored by The Episcopal Church to see the progress being made. Traditional Anglicans, and Christians, will find themselves at odds with this development, because to fit Christianity into the mold essential doctrines will need to be changed. In particular, Jesus has to be changed in order to fit in. This is in fact exactly what is happening, and why the Anglican Church is in crisis.

Anglican Re-Formation

The pressure to conform to the dictates of a new one-world religious movement is resulting in Christians everywhere making a fresh commitment to the essential doctrines of the faith. A great dividing is taking place between those who are taking the path dictated by the spirit of the age, and those committed to the faith once delivered to the saints. Taken together, momentum is building for the unification of the Christian church in a way not seen since its beginning. The dividing walls are coming down, as churches found across the spectrum of genuine Christianity realize that they believe in the same truth of the Gospel, and that truth is under attack. In conclusion, I believe an emerging one-world religion will find itself in conflict with an equally emerging one-world church, comprised of a unified fellowship of Christians of all denominations who hold to the traditional doctrines and practice of the faith.

Throughout the paradigm shifts of western society the Anglican-Ism has survived, giving place to four distinct expressions of faith and practice: evangelical, catholic, charismatic, and liberal. Due to their adherence to the traditional authorities of the premodern era, and their acceptance of the Biblical worldview in general, the first three can be included together under the heading of conservative, or orthodox. In living through the paradigm shift to postmodernity in the West, the conservative camp has continued to diminish both in size and influence, especially in the United States and Canada. Meanwhile, the liberal faction has taken hold of the reins of power, setting their theology and practice to join with the spirit of the age in expanding the postmodern worldview. Albeit, conflict is on the horizon as the conservative expressions found largely in the newly formed Anglican Global South churches are thriving, and have, over time, matured into a force to be reckoned with.

Pluralism, relativism, and tolerance are the new authorities of the postmodern era. In many ways, these represent the ideals of modernity, radicalized, and taken to their logical conclusion. As we find ourselves immersed in the next paradigm shift, Anglican-Ism produces not one clear vision, but in reality two competing visions of what it means to be the church. These visions grow more distinct and organized, visible in the faith communities which embrace, promote and develop them. 1) A liberal postmodern vision authorized by the subjective experience of the self with the Divine, and found mainly in the progressive churches in the West; 2) A conservative orthodox vision authorized by an objective reading of Holy Scripture and visible in the evangelical, Anglo-catholic, and charismatic churches of the Global South. Finally, the Anglican-Ism has come to the crossroads, where simply reasserting that we are all one church because we all share a *Book of Common Prayer* (BCP) will no longer suffice. Indeed, even the commonality of the BCP is challenged by the emergence of new liturgies, which promote theologies further and further afield from a traditional Christian belief.

It is the comprehensiveness, openness, and vitality of the Anglican-Ism that gave rise to this liberal/conservative dichotomy. It is the lack of boundaries and absence of central authority, the high value of autonomy, also found in the mix, which have now created the dilemma we find ourselves in. Which worldview will prevail in the contest for the soul of the Anglican Communion? This question is particularly acute for conservatives, who although in the majority worldwide, have been unable to secure the communion against liberal innovations. Meanwhile, liberals steadily beat the drum of revision, with a commitment to see their will accomplished and a patient strategy designed to wear down their opponents and win the day.

Paradigm to paradigm the Anglican Church has come down through history. The flexibility and resilience of the Anglican-Ism has brought us this far, only to come at last to crisis. It is a crisis that is formulated on the cusp of the next paradigm shift to the one-world era. It is a crisis that must be resolved, that will be resolved one way or another. It is a crisis of two visions: each with its own theology; each with its own practice; each with its own agenda.

Oil and water will not mix, as we shall see in the next chapter.

"Two paths diverged in a wood.
I took the path less traveled by,
and that made all the difference"

—ROBERT FROST

Chapter 3
Two Visions

As we follow the Anglican Church down through the paradigm shifts of history, we can readily observe the development of two separate and distinct visions, each striving for ascendancy. Both seek to answer the question, "What does it mean to be a Christian?" Each promotes its own set of answers, theological beliefs, and accepted practices. One of these visions can be identified as Liberal Protestant Christianity and is commonly called progressive. The other vision is most often referred to as conservative, or Orthodox Christianity, and would consider itself to be apostolic— that is, holding to the original teachings of the apostles.

Two Visions

These two visions are both viable and visible within Anglican Church, but are by no means limited to Anglicans. To the contrary, both are actively being embraced and practiced by congregations and denominations across the whole spectrum of the church universal. Indeed, in our time there has emerged a great competition for the heart and soul of Christendom, and many are beginning to awake to this fact. The question is, "What can be done?"

Every vision springs forth from basic first principles or assumptions about what is real, true, or vitally important. These are found in what are commonly called worldviews. Worldviews give "axiomatic", first answers to the essential questions which confront us in life. Questions such as, why are we here? what is the nature of reality? is there a God? what happens in death? how do we decide right from wrong? Worldviews comprise the foundation upon which a vision is built. Once vision is brought into being, it further influences our perception of what we see and understand. An operating system develops from the lines of code beneath that directs the ideas and practices we are actively engaged in, along with the desire to perpetuate or develop them as time unfolds.

Before we can move forward toward proposal of action, first let us take time to bring each vision into sharper focus. In this manner, we will be able to better ascertain the distinctions between them, the ways in which they contradict one another, and the inherent conflict that comes from both claiming legitimacy. In doing so we will discover that in our time it is no longer sufficient to simply say, "I am a Christian." We must now go further, much further, in explaining what we mean when we say it.

The Liberal Vision

To begin our consideration of how these two visions came into being, let us take a step back to the period of the Enlightenment, a time of transition into the modern era. This is when reason had emerged as the reigning value for mankind, after the bloody wars between Roman Catholic and Protestant religions had left Europe longing for a more sensible way to order society.

During this time the traditional authority vested in the Holy Scriptures and the church lost credibility, and were challenged by a rising objective secularism in the universities, which took the form of an activity know as higher criticism. In response, and perhaps also in participation, a prominent group of German theologians sought to move the residency of Christian faith onto a different foundation-one that could withstand the assault of unbridled reason; one that allowed for modern sensibilities; and one that embraced and affirmed the deeper meanings of our humanity. Chief among these theologians was Friedrich Schleiermacher.

Schleiermacher comes into prominence as a modern theologian in Germany. He was educated in the Moravian school of German Pietist, and as a young man was confronted with a general disdain for religion among his peers. Religion had come to be despised by the educated classes in Germany, with Christianity in particular being discredited by German scholars as historically suspect and scientifically untrue. Schleiermacher sought to answer these critiques and set religion on a new foundation, one that was impervious from attack by the Enlightenment weapons of reason, facts, and knowledge based on scientific method.

In this highly affective environment, Schleiermacher crafted his apology for a more acceptable Christianity in his *Speeches on Religion to its Cultured Despisers*, which based religion in an existential expression of feelings and experience. He drew a sharp distinction between the realm of the intellect, science and knowledge, and the realm of faith, feeling and intuition. For Schleiermacher faith constituted another form of knowing, which touched on the divine in ways not possible by the rational side of our being. Feeling is much more than a passing emotional moment. It is an experience of connection with divine consciousness.[1]

Therefore, the various outward forms of religion—doctrine, dogma, or ritual—are merely human attempts to formalize the experience of the Infinite that is common to all. Religion is not

---

1. Schleiermacher, *Speeches on Religion to its Cultured Despisers*

Two Visions

found through knowledge in the rational sense of the word. Rather it comes to us as a deep feeling—a revelation of the Infinite in the finite. Schleiermacher grounds religion and Christianity in the inner essence, the kernel of human affect, experienced by each person in their own particular individuality. This experience then gives rise to the various corporate expressions of religion, which act as portals to the deeper truth for the novice. The whole of religion only being possible when viewed through an "endless number of forms which must encapsulate every person's experience."[2]

Schleiermacher is considered to be the father of liberalism, and rightly so. By basing theology in the personal experience of the individual, he paved the way for the development of modern liberalism in which the essence of religion is subjective, rather than objective. Revelation is changed from an historical event to an immediate experience. Liberalism emphasizes that we can find God within ourselves, and that the divine kingdom can be identified in the historical process. We find God in the evolutionary process of nature and history, not in the creeds and sacraments of the Church.

Liberalism paints an optimistic picture of the human condition and of history. Since religion is grounded in a subjective experience common to all people, universalism is the logical conclusion. Liberal theology has a powerful appeal to modern mankind as it affirms the validity of all religions and maintains the autonomy of every individual. The dictum of "God within" frees every man and woman from any obligation to objective standards of religious dogma; all are at liberty to define what is right in their own eyes. There is no need to repent and receive forgiveness, as sin is more of a "troubled harmony within ourselves" which destroys our relationship with the divine. Thus, universal acceptance and love of self promote the optimistic growth of human potential in an ever upward spiral of evolution.

In the West, the Anglican/Episcopal Church has maintained an elite social status. The ideology of the culture reaffirmed the theologically liberal presuppositions flowing from the post-enlightenment modern era. Church and culture began a dance of

2. Schleiermacher, *Speeches on Religion to its Cultured Despisers*

affirmation, informing one another while propagating a progressive view of God and human nature. A good example is Episcopal Bishop J.T. Robinson's book, *Honest to God* written in the nineteen sixties. In it he encapsulates a modern critical approach to scripture, and asserts the desirability of redefining, or revising, the doctrines of the Christian faith.

Robinson seeks to express a progressive Christianity that is at one with the surrounding culture. His book is a synthesis of the presuppositions of the Enlightenment, Romanticism, and the reductionist ethics of liberal Protestantism. He embraces the tenets of secular humanism, and infuses them with a wholly immanent concept of God, in order to produce a worldview that is best described as monistic. Authority is transferred to the autonomous self in opposition to the tradition of church and state. Optimism reigns supreme in the ability of human achievement and understanding. As Robinson quotes throughout his book, "Man has come of age."[3]

By embracing the presuppositions of the Enlightenment, Robinson embraces a new worldview. One that is distinctly different from the biblical worldview, and the heart-beat of traditional Christianity. He promotes a monistic, or panentheistic, theology in opposition to the classic distinction between God and creation. He dismantles traditional Christianity, redefining its core components and impregnating them with new meaning. In doing so he retains traditional language and incorporates it into a radically different system of belief.

We have spent some time with J. T. Robinson because he is a pivotal figure who represents the culmination of the liberal vision that began in modernity. *Honest to God* was written on the cusp of the paradigm shift to the postmodern era, and serves as a springboard for those who follow. Continuing the trajectory, others, such as Sallie MacFague and Bishop John Shelby Spong, took the next steps in delivering a revised Christianity made ready and pliable for acceptance into an emerging postmodern ethos.

MacFague draws upon previous uses of mother imagery for God in the writings of female Christian mystics during medieval

---

3. Robinson, *Honest to God*

Two Visions

times and, surprisingly, from insights garnished from near-eastern goddess religions to make her case that God as Mother is a historically valid portrayal. Furthermore, she portrays the Motherhood of God as a metaphor more viably suited for the contemporary sensibility.

The interrelatedness of all life, including God, is the goal to which MacFague aspires. Mother God gives and participates in the life of the world, whereas Father God stands aloof and intervenes only in the process of redemption. "The uneasy feeling many Protestants have about God as the 'ground of all Being arises from the fact that their consciousness is shaped by the demanding father image for which righteousness and not the gift of life is primary. What the father-God gives is redemption from sins; what the mother-God gives is life."[4]

The portrait of God as Mother, who gives birth to and nurtures the world, effectively establishes a monistic doctrine of God's nature. God and the world are indistinct from one another, creation itself being part of God. All of the created order and God are interdependent, one does not exist without the other. MacFague describes the world as being God's body, in a manner best represented as panentheistic. Thus, her theological depiction of creation is radically altered from the traditional understanding.

This revision is clearly in view when the former Episcopal presiding bishop, Katherine Jeffry Schori, prayed to "Mother Jesus" immediately following her consecration.

Bishop Spong shreds Christianity completely with his 12 Thesis:

1. Theism, as a way of defining God, is dead. So most theological God-talk is today meaningless. A new way to speak of God must be found.

2. Since God can no longer be conceived in theistic terms, it becomes nonsensical to seek to understand Jesus as the incarnation of the theistic deity. So, the Christology of the ages is bankrupt.

---

4. MacFague, *Models for God*, 101.

3. The biblical story of the perfect and finished creation from which human beings fell into sin is pre-Darwinian mythology and post-Darwinian nonsense.

4. The virgin birth, understood as literal biology, makes Christ's divinity, as traditionally understood, impossible.

5. The miracle stories of the New Testament can no longer be interpreted in a post-Newtonian world as supernatural events performed by an incarnate deity.

6. The view of the cross as the sacrifice for the sins of the world is a barbarian idea based on primitive concepts of God and must be dismissed.

7. Resurrection is an action of God. Jesus was raised into the meaning of God. It therefore cannot be a physical resuscitation occurring inside human history.

8. The story of the Ascension assumed a three-tiered universe and is therefore not capable of being translated into the concepts of a post-Copernican space age.

9. There is no external, objective, revealed standard writ in scripture or on tablets of stone that will govern our ethical behavior for all time.

10. Prayer cannot be a request made to a theistic deity to act in human history in a particular way.

11. The hope for life after death must be separated forever from the behavior control mentality of reward and punishment. The Church must abandon, therefore, its reliance on guilt as a motivator of behavior.

12. All human beings bear God's image and must be respected for what each person is. Therefore, no external description of one's being, whether based on race, ethnicity, gender or sexual orientation, can properly be used as the basis for either rejection or discrimination.[5]

---

5. Spong, 12 *Theses*

Two Visions

The Conservative Vision

Conservative Christianity draws its strength from the early councils of the church, which by and large defined Orthodox theological beliefs and practices over against false variations and heresies of the time. Deference to the apostles and the Holy Scriptures, taken as inspired in the plain meaning of the text, combined to reinforce the strength of the creeds brought into being through the early councils of the whole church. Church fathers and theologians, such as Augustine of Hippo, Basil the Great, and Thomas Aquinas, contributed further insights to the vision according to their time. Many newer church expressions today, who in fact embody and promote a conservative vision of Christianity, might do well to remember that for centuries the Roman Catholic and Eastern Orthodox expressions kept trust for future generations.

As we have seen, the development of liberal theology came in many ways as a response to the attacks from modern critical thinking. Belief in the Bible, the hierarchy of the church, and the teachings of the church fathers were being ripped to shreds during the time of the Enlightenment by secular scholars who developed a method known as higher criticism. In the rush to reason and scientific method as the new arbiters of objective truth, ancient authorities were cast aside. This included church offices, creeds, and councils, as well as the Bible. Like their liberal counterparts, conservatives also grappled with these challenges and reacted in ways that were not that unpredictable.

In many ways, conservative Christianity began to withdraw from the public sphere. With its credibility threatened, while being castigated in the public sectors of science, commerce, and education, conservatives battened down the hatches within their respective communities. In some cases, they proceeded in forming their own Bible colleges to counter the secular universities. Fundamentalism emerged as a kind of fortress against the assault. Once again conserving, keeping intact, the foundational truths of what it means to be a Christian.

Anglican Re-Formation

Entering the 20th century, we find Karl Barth as an example of a theologian that continued the conservative vision, and gave to it the insights needed for his time. His massive work, *Church Dogmatics*, expounds on the basic doctrines and beliefs held by the Christian church for thousands of years. His conservative stance earned him the title "neo-orthodox"—orthodox in the new modern era. He along with others kept the conservative candle lit on the windowsill of the protestant churches, providing a steadfast critique against the prevalent liberalism of the day. This critique is summed up in a famous quote by Richard Niebuhr: "A God without wrath brought man without sin into a kingdom without judgment through the ministration of a Christ without a cross."[6]

Evangelicals also had their part to play in the continuance of the conservative vision, with resurgence worthy of John Wesley. Billy Graham and his crusade proclaimed the gospel around the United States, and eventually the world. Evangelical colleges, such as Wheaton, Biola, and Westmont, were formed to provide scholarly education which also affirmed faith and belief in the Bible. The evangelical movement came home in the Anglican Church through the ministries of the likes of John Stott and J. I. Packer. In time, Trinity Episcopal School for Ministry was formed in the United States in order to provide theological training grounded in the evangelical/conservative way of belief.

Packer portrays evangelicals as the standard bearers of orthodoxy in the Anglican Church. This is an awesome responsibility, one that carries with it the challenge to confront heretical viewpoints as being unchristian. By recognizing the unity which evangelicals have by means of agreement on the essentials, a solid base for identity can be maintained in the face of such challenges. Above all the seduction of pluralism, under the guise of tolerance, should be avoided by maintaining the uniqueness of Christ and the necessity of the Gospel.

Evangelicalism is grounded on a cluster of six controlling convictions, each of which is regarded as being true, of vital importance, and grounded in scripture. These are not purely doctrinal, if

---

6. Niebuhr, *The Kingdom of God in America*

Two Visions

this term is understood to refer purely to a set of objective truths; they are also existential, in that they affirm the manner in which the believer is caught up in a redemptive and experiential encounter with the living Christ. These six fundamental convictions can be set out as follows:

Six Evangelical Fundamentals

1. The Supremacy of Holy Scripture
   —*the source of knowledge of God and a guide to Christian living.*

2. The Majesty of Jesus Christ
   —*both as incarnate God and Lord and as the Savior of sinful humanity.*

3. The Lordship of the Holy Spirit
   —*third person of the Trinity who guides us in all truth*

4. The Necessity of Conversion
   —*personal decision to accept Christ as Savior*

5. The Priority of Evangelism
   —*for both individual Christians and the church as a whole*

6. The Importance of Fellowship
   —*Christian community is vital for spiritual nourishment, fellowship and growth*[7]

Evangelical is a term by which a rather broad section of the church would identify itself with today, especially in the West. While forms of worship may vary between contemporary and traditional styles, and doctrines may differ, the Six Evangelical Fundamentals are a set of core beliefs. Agreement on these fundamental tenets of the faith unites Anglican evangelicals with those in other denominations, promoting a value of ecumenical unity. At the risk of over simplification, evangelicals claim faithfulness

---

7. McGrath, *Evangelical Distinctives*, 55–56.

to apostolic teaching as the criteria by which to judge an authentic expression of the church.

And so, the conservative vision has remained viable in the Anglican Church and throughout worldwide Christianity. While all the while alongside, the liberal vision has grown in strength, character, and adherents. As we come to the second half of the twentieth century, both begin to crystallize in their assertion of what it means to be a Christian: liberals by adapting to the contemporary culture around them; conservatives reasserting truth from the past.

The Two Visions

The liberal vision, sometimes called "catholic modernism" soon became ensconced in the Episcopal seminaries, where, for the following decades, clergy were formed and indoctrinated. Upon graduation, these same clergy then were placed into ministry positions in the local congregations and dioceses, where the liberal vision was then presented as the gospel. By the turn of the century, 2000, Western Anglicanism had become for the most part synonymous with this liberal vision. This is especially true of The Episcopal Church, but also many of the western provinces in general, i.e. England, Ireland, Canada, etc.

While the liberal vision was gaining ground in the West, the conservative orthodox vision, planted by missionaries in previous eras in Africa, Asia, and South America had grown up into a vibrant new force in the Anglican Communion. The Global South had come of age. The orthodox vision maintained a conservative position on "the faith once delivered to the saints." This phrase contains the understanding that Holy Scripture and the traditional interpretation thereof form the bedrock of doctrine and practice for the church; promotes the acceptance of a plain reading of scripture as authoritative; and upholds a biblical worldview unfiltered and unmodified by the modern or postmodern paradigm.

The two visions, liberal and orthodox, flow from two competing worldviews, postmodern and biblical. The postmodern worldview presents a closed system of the universe. This view maintains all that exists, either natural or spiritual, is contained in and part of the system. There is no objective reality, or God, that stands above or apart. Creation and creator are one, and our own experience as conscious human beings is what determines what is true. The biblical worldview declares creation and creator distinct from one another. The physical universe exists and is contingent upon the spiritual realm that transcends it. God is objective, above and beyond, and he alone is the final arbiter of what is true. Our part as human beings is to receive his word and come to know him on a journey through this world and on into eternity.

It is interesting to consider the difference between these competing streams of theological expression. Coming down through the modern era and into Postmodernity, the liberal vision has remained lively. That is to say the liberal worldview has continued to develop and morph toward maturity, seeking to engage and draw into itself the populace, the world, and the culture. In short, it is actively engaged in persuasion, and continually producing the next representative. Can the same be said for orthodoxy? Certainly, this is a question worth pondering as we move ahead.

By and large those who hold to the biblical orthodox beliefs have remained faithful and true, even if struggling somewhat to develop relevancy to the surrounding culture. Those who hold to the liberal beliefs have embraced a state of flux—changing, adapting, and revising to the culture so as to be spiritual in the world. These two different systems of beliefs now vie for the heart of Christianity, each providing a radically different answer to the question, "What does it mean to be a Christian?" Within the Anglican Communion we see them both on display and in conflict with one another.

I have heard it said that the United States and England are two nations separated by a common language. For, even though both share a common heritage from the past, today the words and the meanings are set in the context of different cultures, different histories, and a matrix of knowing and perceiving the world that is peculiar to each country. The language sounds the same, but much of what is said means something completely different.

The same holds true for liberal and conservative Anglicans. We are two churches separated by a common language. Although we share a common heritage, the priorities and practice of our faith are set in the context of different theologies, alternative views of the surrounding culture, and a matrix of knowing and perceiving God and the world that is peculiar to each.

Much of what is said in conversation with each other sounds the same, but the meanings are substantially different. Each community may be able to hear the words of the other, but in the end both walk away perplexed not understanding what the other really meant. Perplexion turns to confusion, confusion to frustration, and frustration to anger. We get angry because the others just don't seem to get it. We seem to say the same thing, but then act in ways that are radically different.

Naturally, the situation is not as simple as this. A whole spectrum exists in between the extreme left and the extreme right. Individuals, parishes, and dioceses consist of different mixes and opinions. This postmodern tendency to customize our own religious beliefs adds to the complexity and the confusion. Nevertheless, in the final analysis there remain two distinct theological systems, two religious expressions, which are distinct and irreconcilable.

At present both remain conjoined, two churches separated by a common language, the language of Anglican Christianity. Both uphold the *Book of Common Prayer* as the standard of worship. Both ascribe to tradition, reason, and scripture as the Anglican way. Both claim to be legitimate heirs of the Anglican tradition. Indeed, both may be justified in doing so, as the Anglican stream has provided a place of nurture for each.

Both theological expressions purport to uphold the truth of the Gospel. Both affirm the authority of Holy Scripture. Both hold up Jesus Christ as Savior. Both even maintain that they are orthodox. Like the surface of a lake on a still afternoon, each reflects the surrounding landscape of Anglicanism, in an illusion of unity. But, beneath the surface there is a great divide.

In order to plunge into the depths and see clearly the division that resides there, one must ask questions that break through

Two Visions

the surface mirage, questions that are penetrating. For example, we may ask, "Is Jesus Christ the Savior?" All will answer, "Yes." But if we ask, "Who is Jesus?" "What do we mean by the Christ?" or, "What is the nature of sin and salvation?" Very different answers will begin to emerge. These answers form the theological presuppositions, which in turn order the faith and practice of each respective church community.

Who is Jesus? What is the Gospel? How does Holy Scripture have authority? What is sin? Morality? Is God independent from the universe, or interdependent with it? Is God a personal transcendent being, or a divine immanent force? These questions penetrate the idyllic surface of statements which all claim to adhere to. Beneath the surface, we are faced with answers from two separate and distinct theological systems. These systems may be cohesive, in and of themselves, but are radically different from one another.

Once the surface is broken, like a scuba diver we begin to see clearly what lies beneath. Two distinct visions of what it means to be an Anglican, indeed even what it means to be a Christian, have emerged, and there is a great divide between them. This divide will not be breached by simply talking it over in the common language of the surface. Such conversation is merely representative, it simply does not convey the meanings that reside in the depth. The only way this division can be overcome, would be if one or the other abandons their theological presuppositions.

Will this happen? Will liberal Anglicans abandon their commitment to promoting Gay—Lesbian—Bisexual—Transgender inclusiveness, a peace and justice Gospel, and the acceptance of all faiths as equivalent paths to God? Will conservative Anglicans abandon their commitment to morality based on an objective scriptural standard, Jesus as the exclusive means of salvation, and a Gospel that proclaims the need to convert others to Christianity?

Simply answered, *no*!

Neither liberals nor conservatives will abandon the foundations of their faith as they see it. Whole lives and whole communities of faith are formed and committed to these two increasingly distinct and separate systems of belief. For either of them to cast aside these foundations would be to abandon their understanding of God, and, along with it, the community that is formed around that understanding.

And so, we remain divided, two churches, two theologies, separated by a common language. The division will only become greater as time goes on. Unless we honestly acknowledge the divide and embrace a realistic solution, lack of understanding, frustration, and anger will continue to escalate. Eventually, the Anglican Communion will disintegrate as a worldwide body.

The only way to resolve the conflict is through re-formation. In order to maintain integrity and fulfill their respective visions, liberals and conservatives must each reform into their own distinctive communities of faith. Attempting to force one side to capitulate to the other will only result in the shredding of all. Through its current actions, The Episcopal Church U.S.A. seems to have recognized this, and is actively seeking to grab as much as possible before the breakup gets under way. Conservatives also have followed suit, gathering multiple jurisdictions together to form the new province of the Anglican Church in North America. Yet, I am arguing that the time for waiting is long past. We who are participants in the orthodox vision need to initiate action before it is too late.

The Great Divide

In the previous chapter, we considered the historical paradigm shifts in the West, especially in relation to the Anglican-Ism. These transformations on the grand scale are typically preceded by an emerging crisis, which gradually develops and begins to assert stain on the accepted norms. Finally, a breaking point is reached, then the shift takes place ushering in the new era. The Anglican Church itself has now reached such a breaking point.

The Anglican Communion is living through a paradigm shift of its own. The crisis within Anglican-Ism has been developing for a long time, and now must be resolved. Yet, the existing instruments of unity are insufficient to deal with the problems that now confront us as a church. They must be modified, enhanced, or changed

Two Visions

altogether in order to resolve the crisis and set the Anglican Church in proper alignment. Re-formation is needed if we are to be effective in our proclamation of the Gospel in the new one-world era.

In a nutshell, the crisis is a conflict between two competing worldviews: The biblical worldview and the postmodern worldview. Worldviews contain the axis of belief, especially religious beliefs, from the answers they provide to questions regarding the nature of God, the universe, and mankind. Both the biblical and the postmodern worldviews present and promote a vision of faith and practice—a liberal vision and a conservative vision. These visions have both grown up in the Anglican-Ism, and thus can both claim to be legitimate heirs. Yet, they are distinct from one another. Each is radically different in the literal meaning of the word radical—at the root. The two are incompatible and irreconcilable. The crisis being, they both seek to control the whole of the Anglican Church in the twenty-first century. Only one can succeed.

At its heart, the Anglican crisis is a Christian crisis. The problems on display within the Anglican Communion have been likened to a long slow motion train wreck. However, the screeching wheels and crunching metal is not limited to Anglicans. The church universal is facing the same problems and dynamics in our time. The question posed to the church is simply this, "What does it mean to be a Christian?"

Within the Anglican-Ism, the two visions promote two very different answers to the question. This is confusing because both claim to represent Anglican/Christian belief. The confusion is deepened by the fact that both utilize language which is recognizable as distinctly Christian. The two visions cannot be reconciled, and they can no longer be maintained in cozy proximity under the banner of one church body. The liberal vision of the western provinces has supporters who are politically astute, well financed, and deeply committed to fulfilling their agenda. The heresy which they promote, like leaven, could permeate the whole of Anglican-ism.

The great divide in the Anglican stream of Christianity is upon us. The division, which is already a reality beneath the surface, is becoming visible and tangible to all. Common language does not make the English into Americans, nor Americans into English. Neither will it make liberals into conservative Anglicans, nor conservative Anglicans into liberal ones.

The Anglican Communion is in crisis. The time for denial is over. The day is at hand when all must choose to stand on one side of the divide or the other. Orthodox believers must initiate the Anglican re-formation of the twenty-first century, to restore and realign the historic Anglican-Ism, reclaiming a genuine expression of Christian faith for the new paradigm. Let us turn then to a deeper consideration of the crisis, the problems, and the possible solutions.

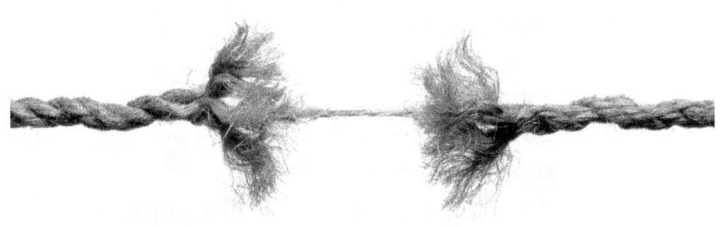

"No one can serve two masters,
for either he will hate the one and love the other,
or he will be devoted to the one and despise the other."

—MATTHEW 6:24

Chapter 4
Crisis

The two visions of Christian faith and practice described in the previous chapter represent the active expression of radically different theologies. Two opposing worldviews that are each striving for ascendancy within the same community—namely the church. In such a situation, a crisis is inevitable. It is a crisis that we now find ourselves in the midst of today: of beliefs and values; of polity and authority; and of relationship and community.

In some ways, this current situation is not unlike the crisis of Arianism, which gripped the early church. At heart, what was at stake was the very identity of the Christian community. The answer to the question, "What does it mean to be a Christian?" or of equal import "Who is Jesus?" Arias promoted a different view of Jesus Christ, one that was more acceptable to the prevailing culture of the time. His view made more sense, seemed more reasonable, and was more affirming to humanity. Jesus was a man just like us. He was a created being. As a result, Arianism was very persuasive. Gradually, this alternative viewpoint began to permeate through the greater community of faith. The Roman Empire was on the way to becoming Arian. Missionaries were even sent to the Balkans bearing this gospel message.

However, the opposing worldview of Trinitarian faith, represented by Athanasius, could not yield, mold, nor adapt to the new ideal. It was impossible. Not because of sheer stubbornness, but because of genuine commitment to the veracity of scripture. Pressure mounted against Athanasius to compromise for the sake of the unity of the church. He was told, "The world is against you," to which he replied, "Then I am against the world." Hence, we have the famous quotation, "Athanasius contra mundum!" It is the truth that must be upheld.

This crisis culminated in the Council of Nicaea 325AD. There Athanasius, and those others with him, prevailed, and the foundation of Christian belief was set on the solid rock of the authority of Holy Scripture, and formulated into a creed of confession. The church continues to declare the Nicene Creed as the cornerstone of our belief to this day.

Like Arianism, the liberal worldview today, with its revised understandings of God and humanity, has slowly and steadily permeated the Church in the west. This expression seeks to befriend the surrounding culture, and draw insights from a plurality of sources. This makes more sense to the world we live in, seems more reasonable, more affirming to our mutual humanity. Yet, at heart it promotes a radical change of identity to all who call themselves Christian. What does it mean to be a Christian? Who is Jesus? A very different set of answers are being offered.

As an Anglican priest and rector of St. Luke's Anglican Church, I have experienced firsthand the unfolding of the liberal-conservative schism being played out between The Episcopal Church (TEC) and their Anglican counterparts. At the heart of the matter, there resides a theological divide, which is irreconcilable. It all boils down to two different visions for Christian faith and practice. Each has their own distinct set of core beliefs. Each have their own set of accepted practices. Each provides a definition of what it means to be a Christian, especially in our time.

Let me offer a brief comparative analysis based upon facts, which are easily verifiable.

The Liberal Episcopal Church teaches and promotes:

- Many Ways: all major religions provide equal access to God. Jesus is only the prominent way of Western culture.

- Authority of Spiritual Experience: the subjective understanding of each person is the basis for deciding what is true and/or morally acceptable. The Bible may provide good examples, but does not have objective authority for all generations.

- A Revised Understanding of God, Jesus Christ, and Human Nature: God is a divine spirit found within the physical universe; Jesus Christ is a man that fully accessed this divine spirit in conscious human form, and thus is our prime example; Human Nature is inherently good. Since we are made in God's image, the divine spirit resides in every person. We are all part of God.

- Human Sexuality: affirmed in all the various expressions, according to one's own personal self-identity.

To be clear, I am not suggesting that every member of the Episcopal Church wholly ascribes to the beliefs listed above. But their church as a body has embraced this new form of revised Christianity. As we have discussed previously, it is taught in their seminaries, and their bishops are actively promoting it. Look up the following examples online: Bishop Swing's United Religions Initiative; Presiding Bishop Schori's Prayer to Mother Jesus; Bishop Gene Robinson's Affirmation of GLBT Lifestyle; Bishop Jon Bruno, Apology to Hindus for Christian Mission.

In contrast Anglicans join with Catholics, Orthodox, Evangelicals, and others in maintaining the original Christian beliefs taught by the Apostles.

Conservative Anglicans teach and promote:

- One Way: through Jesus alone we are restored in our relationship with God and with one another. He is the fulfillment of all religions.

- Authority of Holy Scripture: The basis of deciding what is true and morally acceptable is given to us in the objective authority of God's word. This remains true for all generations.

- A Traditional Understanding of God, Jesus Christ, and Human Nature: God is the creator of the universe and remains distinct from it; Jesus is both human and divine, the one and only Son of God whose death and resurrection brings us new life. Human Nature is inherently sinful. God's image remains, but it is broken by our willful rejection of His ways.

- Human Sexuality: Affirmed exclusively in marriage between one man and one woman. All other sexual expressions and practices are outside the boundaries set by God.

It is not enough to claim "We say the Nicene Creed every Sunday" as evidence of Christian belief. One must ask the deeper question, "What exactly do you mean by the words you are reciting?" Episcopalians have embraced the postmodern spirit of the age in an attempt to be relevant to the culture. In doing so, they have changed the core beliefs of Christian faith at the very roots. This revision then becomes a pseudo Christianity, which is radically opposed to the original. The two cannot be reconciled by simply saying, "Let's all be friends." We no longer worship the same God.

Those who remain committed to the orthodox worldview cannot change, adapt, nor yield to this new religious movement. It is impossible. Since we are both vying for the same thing, the identity of the church, the crisis has come.

It has been a slowly developing crisis, which began almost unnoticed. The conflict, or set of conflicts, has grown steadily through the end of the twentieth century, and now continue into the twenty-first. The underlying causes finally came to a head within the Anglican Church in 2003 with the election, and subsequent consecration, of Vicki Gene Robinson as Bishop of New Hampshire, the Episcopal Church. The first openly practicing homosexual appointed to be a bishop in the church.

Let us take a moment to consider this crisis, the conflicts that brought us here, and the stages and strategies engaged in as a result. In my view there are four distinct possibilities of response to the situation. Some responses which come naturally, and some which require more effort, determination, and clarity of thinking to bring about. The four are:

1. Denial
2. Reconciliation
3. Détente
4. Re-formation

Denial

Grandpa used to say, "There has never been a problem I couldn't solve without a healthy dose of pure denial." Grandpa was wrong. Just ask Grandma. Denial does not solve problems, it does not resolve conflicts and it does not take us out of crisis. In fact, it only makes matters worse, prolonging the inevitable. Yet, denial often remains as a preeminent response to difficulties that we find ourselves in, especially difficulties in relationships with one another. Why? Perhaps because it seems easier, and may be indeed so in the short run: perhaps because we don't like confrontation; it makes us uncomfortable. In the life of the church, time progresses slowly. Church time is slow time, so we are not pressed to find a resolution quickly or do the hard work of honesty. Genuine honesty is the opposite of denial.

Denial is an immediate human reaction, and it has been on display as the preeminent strategy throughout the current Anglican crisis. In the early stages when liberal pseudo-Christian doctrine began to permeate the seminaries and pulpits in the West, conservative response was muted. Certainly, there was disagreement and a certain wagging of heads. There was a commitment to pray for those who were off track, but not recognition that the communion itself was being threatened. Many thought that even though there are some fringe teachings in seminaries, and even though there are some bishops like Spong who are out there, this does not affect our worship or our communion together. This does not affect our doctrine. After all, doctrine is set in *the Book of Common Prayer*, and that has not changed.

Liberals declared the highest principle to be unity, and who can argue against that? Schism is the eighth deadly sin. There are many ways of interpreting scripture, who can know for certain which is right? Let everyone decide for themselves. Let's all stay together, for that is what is most important. We all say the same creed; therefore, we all believe the same thing. And so, the conflicts simmered, and the crisis grew deeper.

When Gene Robinson was elected as the first openly practicing gay bishop, it was time for a reality check. Orthodox and Global South Anglicans issued a warning against his consecration. "Don't do this or you will tear the fabric of the communion at the deepest level"—a good attempt at genuine honesty. In fact, the fabric was already torn. The foundation was split in two. Underneath the house, there already existed a great chasm. Robinson only opened a portal to make it visible.

Denial continued. On the right: this gay bishop thing is an anomaly; it won't happen again. After all it only affects one diocese, New Hampshire. TEC will listen, heed the warnings, and see the error of their ways. This crisis will not get progressively worse. And, on the left: we are sorry you are hurt by our actions. There will be a moratorium on further consecrations like this one. After all, we continue to affirm the 1998 Dar es Salam accords which affirmed biblical sexual morality as the agreed upon standard for the communion. From both sides it would seem that there is no acknowledgement of the common use of language with inherently different meanings. "Why do we say the same things, but it does not solve the crisis?"

The strategy from the liberal side has been to buy time to allow further permeation of their revised doctrines, by continuing to deny the problem even exists. "Why can't we be friends?" Their trump card is unity, which they use to propel the crisis down through time to give space for pseudo-Christianity to take over.

The strategy from the orthodox side has been to engage in talking. Let's talk it out. Once the liberals understand what they are doing, and how it is affecting our common life, then they will repent. They will change their actions when we talk to them, and declare our position. Let us take a stand for truth, and truth will prevail. We can persuade TEC to repent. Their trump card is truth, which they use to try to lever the wayward back into the fold.

The highest principle of unity comes into conflict with the highest principle of truth. Which position has been the most effective so far?

At its heart the crisis is a crisis of authority—spiritual authority. In particular, the authority of Holy Scripture and, more specifically, what do we mean by that phrase. As discussed in the last chapter, both liberals and conservatives invoke the authority of scripture, using the same language but meaning something completely different. The way in which liberals and conservatives understand the inspiration and authority of scripture, what each means when they use the terms, and how it applies to the practice of faith makes all the difference.

This crisis of authority fomented is exacerbated by the division over the basic tenets of biblical interpretation. Each has a fundamentally different understanding of what the Bible is, and how it is to be applied to the community of the church. Such misunderstanding can hardly even begin to provide the means for a conversation on the matter, much less be a starting point for the two sides to find agreement and reconciliation. Conservatives and liberals have each set a chief cornerstone of authority upon which their respective communities are built, and the two are in opposition to one another.

Reconciliation

As the Anglican Communion wrestles with the two visions previously described, the proponents of each have set in motion their own particular solution to the conflict. From the liberal camp comes a plea for reconciliation, while conservatives have asserted the need for an Anglican covenant. As solutions to the Anglican crisis, both are woefully inadequate, and in fact have no chance of success. Each offers a false hope, which only serves to propel the conflict further into the future. Such a time delay works to the advantage of the liberal vision, but against those who desire a renewal of the traditional Christian faith.

Reconciliation is hard to argue with. As Christians, we believe that Jesus Christ has reconciled us to God, and given to us the ministry of reconciliation. That is to say that the church is to be God's agent on earth—bearing the good news of his wonderful offer to all the world. This is reconciliation set in a biblical context, describing a restored relationship between God and mankind.

The principles of reconciliation may also be applied in other less theological contexts as well: husbands and wives may be reconciled to each other following marital strife; countries may reconcile their differences prior to warfare; even bank statements need to be reconciled and restored to proper order. Thus, in principle reconciliation removes obstacles, restores relationship, and puts things back into proper order. Therefore, the promotion of reconciliation by TEC as a solution to the Anglican dilemma, sounds at first to be the reasonable, and indeed, Christian approach. However, to see clearly, we must understand and examine the context to which reconciliation is being applied.

As mentioned, there are many situations theological, personal, and practical where reconciliation is appropriate, but there are also times when reconciliation is impossible, and absolutely wrong: an abused wife must not reconcile with a violent husband, good cannot be reconciled with evil; peace with war; fraud and embezzlement with honesty and integrity. There exist moral absolutes which must not be surrendered for the sake of that which opposes them, or reconciliation becomes compromise.

Returning to the theological context, heresy cannot be reconciled with truth. Yet, this is precisely what the liberals and TEC are seeking to accomplish.

Throughout Holy Scripture reconciliation with God is set in contradistinction with reconciliation with the world—"no one can serve two masters"[1]—"what fellowship has light with darkness"[2]—"you shall have no other gods before me."[3] The reconciliation promoted by TEC is a false solution, precisely because the principle is being applied to a situation regarding truth and heresy. Invoking the principle of the Via Media, this approach attempts to resolve the conflict by mediating a compromise. Yet, God has never allowed for such a compromise when it comes to following him, especially regarding his person, his plan, or his people. In short, God does not compromise with sin.

When seen in this light, the solution of reconciliation waged by TEC becomes nothing less than a strategy utilized for the accomplishment of their own agenda—the victory of the liberal vision. After all, who can argue with reconciliation? It sounds so biblical, so loving and true. Therefore, the very use of the word causes Christians to engage with the process, and they are sucked in to a never-ending dialogue bent on compromise and capitulation. "We must continue to dialogue until we understand one another and can be reconciled." In other words, until conservatives compromise and accept the liberal vision as the status quo. Buyer beware! Genuine reconciliation is not possible in this context, no matter how appealing it looks, or is made to sound, because God's truth is lost. Scriptural reconciliation with God always requires repentance and obedience to His ways, not the sinful promotion of the self and the ways of man in the name of religion.

While the liberal strategy of reconciliation seeks to use a biblical principle to force a compromise of truth, conservatives have

1. Matthew 6:24
2. 2 Corinthians 6:14
3. Exodus 20:3

put forth their own solution to safeguard it known as The Anglican Covenant. Frustrated by years of complicity and innuendo on the part of the liberal provinces, Global South Anglicans felt the need for a definitive statement of belief, which all who purport to be Anglican must subscribe to. The Anglican Covenant is in concept a confession of the faith once delivered to the saints—a statement of the core beliefs of the Anglican Church. It is believed that once a covenant is established, order will be restored to the communion. Provinces will self select as to who remains and who departs, because all will be required to ascribe to the covenant in order to be considered part of the Anglican Communion. In a sense, we will all be reconciled as a communion by affirming the covenant together.

As many have pointed out, one of the primary reasons for the current crisis is that there is presently no central authority within the collection of provinces of the worldwide Anglican Church. Each is autonomous unto itself. There is no pope, no council of bishops, nor a committee that can make a judicial ruling regarding either faith or practice, as applicable to the whole. Rather than establish such authority, the Anglican Covenant extends a long process of statements, reports, communiqués, and conferences that have done nothing to address the real issue—namely a new heretical movement which seeks to supplant the Christian faith in Anglicanism. As discussed previously, this crisis is a conflict between two competing worldviews: postmodern and biblical.

Therefore, as a solution to the crisis of Anglicanism, the Anglican Covenant is dead on arrival. It is doomed to the same fate that claimed the effectiveness of its' predecessors, including Lambeth '98, the Windsor Report, Dar es Salaam, and even Holy Scripture itself. All have been taken down and tied in knots by the relativism that operates as a core principle of the liberal vision. Subjective interpretation rules out any possibility for agreement upon a written doctrinal covenant. Even if such a document was written with amazing clarity and unparalleled acumen, multiple and vagrant interpretations will be pried, cajoled, and twisted forth from the subjective understanding of those who are invested in making the covenant serve their own agenda. Remember, meaning is not found in the words of the text, the reader imports their own meaning into it. This is standard operation within the liberal theology of TEC, subjective interpretation has authority in matters regarding faith and practice, and especially regarding anything that is written. In the end the Anglican Covenant will be meaningless, because any and every possible meaning will be derived from it, and attached to it by the liberals.

That said, I must add that the covenant holds some promise as a foundation for a new Anglican Fellowship. Before casting the covenant out altogether, it is necessary to state the great benefit that it does make available, especially for the purposes of re-formation for the orthodox Anglican churches. The beauty and strength of the covenant resides in the clarity which it brings in expressing the biblical world view. The covenant is foundational as a means of binding together like minded orthodox Anglicans worldwide. It provides the confession of faith vital for genuine unity based in truth. However, as we shall discuss, the covenantal statement is not able to accomplish the task alone. What is also required are clear boundaries, central authority, and a certified method of interpretation.

Détente

The stages we are discussing in regards to the crisis that has now fomented in the Anglican communion is not unlike the process that many marriages go through in seeking to work through the difficulties in an intimate relationship. First denial, the problems do not exist, or they will go away if we just ignore them. When that does not work, counseling is the next step. This is the attempt at reconciliation of difficulties through mediation. As a priest, this is often the stage when a couple arrives in my office. Typically, the crisis is upon them in the form of one or the other stating, "I want a divorce!" Various principles can be taught, and exercises assigned in an attempt to break through the stone walls, sometime with success—other times not.

When denial has been in vain, and reconciliation fruitless, the next stage in managing the crisis becomes détente. The decision is made, either consciously or unconsciously, to just tough it out. The idea is that this is a good as it gets. Things are not going to change, and besides it is just taking too much energy to try to work things out. Energy that could be expended on other parts of life which each of the parties value-whether or not the other values them as well no longer matters.

Détente is a kind of truce. You live your way and I will live my way, and we agree not to harass one another, or try to change one another to our point of view. We have tried to do so and it did not work, and it has proven to be not worth the fight. Instead, we will continue in our association together, because that is important.

We will never agree on the truth, but must maintain unity, or at least the appearance of unity, for that appearance gives us an assurance of stability. Also, that appearance maintains our sense of respectability to the world around us. Of course, all of this is merely a façade covering the irreconcilable differences beneath.

Détente is not all that different from denial. Both leave the main issues and the underlying causes of those issues intact. It comes from a lack of will to take action. At this stage of the crisis, the contestants pull back into their respective corners, like boxers who have grown weary through the rounds of a heavyweight fighting match. They seek solace and strength from their supporters—a chance to breathe and apply salve to the wounds. As the fight continues to wait in the ring, they become reluctant to step back in for further punishment, and may simply begin to dance around each other rather than continue the fight.

The above analogy is especially fitting when we observe the state of the whole Anglican Communion at this time. Since the crisis began, we have been through round after round of effort in seeking to overcome the opposition. This has brought us to a time of détente. Liberals have drawn up into their corners, which by the way occupy most of the main offices within the structure of the existing Anglican Communion. Their strategy is to marginalize the orthodox, and paralyze further attempts to effect change. Not to be undone, conservatives/orthodox have moved to create their own alternative structures of the Global Anglican Fellowship. Nevertheless, all remain as participates in the Anglican Communion as a whole. Certainly, not all consider themselves in communion with one another, but nevertheless all remain in association. It is regularly reported by the world at large, "There is no schism in the Anglican Communion." This means we are viewed as being together as one, and the appearance of respectability is maintained. The facade remains intact.

This stage of détente can be clearly evidenced in the functions and events of the communion at large, as well as in the actions of the recognized leaders and "instruments of unity." Take for example the last Lambeth conference, an event that occurs every ten years, and draws together the bishops and archbishops of the entire communion for a meeting of minds and faith at Lambeth palace in England. In the months prior to the last event in 2008, the Archbishop of Canterbury, Rowan Williams, consistently took the position in his statements and writings that all simply needed to live together. That is to say, don't try to fix the problem, because it just takes too much energy. Indeed, Williams' essays are so dense as to form a kind of détente in and of themselves.

When the conference was finally convened, the respective combatants arrived with their own corners already staked out. Each brought with them a team of support, and joined with the others of like mind. The theme of the conference, as set by liberals who control the agenda, was Indaba. Indaba being an African word which signifies the action of taking to one another. The idea and practice of Indaba is that those who do not know each other, those who have different points of view, even those who are in conflict with each other, can simply gather together talk and listen. Thereby understand each other. The bishops came, they Indaba-ed together, and they understood nothing was changed and nothing was going to change. Following the conference the crisis continued as before, in the stage of détente. I would argue that this is the stage we continue in to this day—Indaba forever.

To be fair to the principle of détente, a time of pulling back from active conflict can at times be beneficial in moving toward a resolution of the crisis. As long as pulling back doesn't turn into sitting down. A time of truce can often give place for the hard work needed to move combatants from the ring to back outside the arena, where they can go on living their lives. Sometimes détente gives a chance for diplomacy to work, and mutually agreed upon solutions to be put into effect. In certain situations, or circumstances, this can be the case. But, is this something that can take place in Anglicanism or Christianity as a whole? Can détente provide a way forward when we are dealing with a crisis that envelopes the very heart and soul of Christian faith? As discussed in the last chapter the answer is simply, *no*!

Re-Formation

Denial—Reconciliation—Détente are all merely stopgap measures that propel the crisis onward down through time. They are not bringing resolution. The healthy solution is the proper setting of boundaries, and the enforcement of discipline. Only this will undo the false dichotomy between unity and truth, and set the Anglican Communion back on the right foundation. Unity based on adherence to truth. The Apostolic truth found in the Holy Scripture. Rather than the incessant talking of Indaba, we need to take action. We need re-formation.

Re-formation is often thought of as synonymous with schism. Certainly, the protestant reformation resulted in the splintering of the church into many different groups. But, this does not necessarily need to be the case. The pressing need to restore our common life back to its biblical roots, calls for us to re-form our fellowships in such a way that we gather the fragments back together in a cohesive whole. The process is not unlike the remodeling of a house. The foundation must first be shored up and leveled where needed. Some walls are chosen to remain, some are torn down. New doors and windows may be added, while old ones that have openings no longer desired are closed up. In the end, a home emerges that now fulfills the purposes needed and releases the energy of the family who lives there. The Anglican-Ism needs a new house to dwell in. It is up to us to build it.

The problems that underlie the crisis are often overlooked in a passionate debate about the symptoms. Solutions proposed and discussed along the way come from within the dysfunctional system itself. The attempt to unravel the mess while utilizing the same processes, assumptions, polity, and methods that created the crisis to begin with is doomed to fail. Failure from my point of view means the liberal postmodern worldview will eventually take over.

The problem is not the "gay issue." The problem is the theological grid—first principles, presuppositions, and premises—that allow the gay issue to be an issue in the first place. At heart is a theology of monism which is the belief or understanding that God and the universe are one. Rather than a classic Christian belief in a transcendent God who created the universe, yet is separate and distinct from it. In the monistic world-view God and universe are interconnected and interdependent upon one another. God is changing and evolving and the universe is changing and evolving. God is dependent upon and contained within the physical order; the physical order is dependent upon and contained within God. The older theological term for this is pantheism—meaning God within the world; the newer more sophisticated expression is panentheism—meaning the world is within God. It is important to note that this is the view held by many Eastern religions, like the Hindus, who understand a divine spiritual reality that undergirds all of the physical reality with which we interact.

Monism is one of the basic tenets of the postmodern paradigm, and lays the foundation for the principles of pluralism and tolerance that follow. The acceptance of monism as the chief corner stone of a theological grid allows for the promotion of all religions as equal paths to God. They are like independent oil wells of the spiritual life that drill down to tap into the divine reservoir waiting underneath all. In a sense this is very much the viewpoint of the liberal "Christian" thinkers of modernity. Paul Tillich, remember, describes God as "the Ground of all Being", teaching a radicalized immanence that is essentially the same as monism. This worldview leads to radically different conclusions to the basic questions of; who or what is God? Who is Jesus? What is the nature of humanity? Sin? Salvation? Church? Spirit? and so on. If God, the divine reality is within all things, including human beings, how then can a loving sexual relationship between two men, or between two women be constituted as sinful, or morally wrong. Or for that matter between a man and several wives in polygamy, or two couples joining in intimacy with each other in polyamory. The Christian church would be wrong to quickly dismiss this theological grid as irrelevant or non-threatening, for it continues to be proven very influential in our time, and is quickly becoming the foundation for the emerging one world religion.

The historic opportunity for re-formation and revival is slowly passing by. Rather than denial, attempts at reconciliation, and/or détente, what is needed is action. Action taken in the formation of an Anglican Council, one given the mandate to discern truth from error, good from evil, and one that has the authority to act accordingly. Historically this is exactly what the church did at the Council of Nicaea. What then is the process, specifically, for the Anglican Communion to act with the same vigor and results as the early church acted? The discussion above has been more or less theoretical. Let us move on to a consideration of the actions and events required to affect such a reaffirmation of Christian faith in the Anglican expression in which we participate—noting from the onset that such a reaffirmation will in fact result also in a re-formation of the Anglican-Ism as well. Thus, as we turn toward the next chapter, "Anglican Re-Formation," we are in actuality beginning a discussion of the need and process for re-formation within the Anglican Church, and extending beyond from there to worldwide Christianity.

"I am like a man throwing matches at a haystack,
Hoping that it will light a blaze."

—FR. JACK ESTES

Chapter 5
Anglican Re-Formation

Since the time of the Protestant Reformation, the Anglican Church has nestled comfortably between the shores of the catholic and protestant expressions of Christian belief. The famous "Via Media", the middle way, beckons to those who find satisfaction in its appeal to a comprehensive approach to Christian faith and practice. The Anglican Church has maintained a balanced tradition which holds onto the essentials, while allowing for a grace filled approach to much of religious life which is considered peripheral, or at least preferential.

For centuries this middle way has held true. The genius of the Anglican-Ism in allowing for differences, while asserting minimalist dogma, has charted a safe course through the religious conflicts of the Enlightenment and Modernity. Anglican comprehensiveness assured a certain liberty from strife, by providing a measured autonomy for the provinces which circumvent the globe. Yet, it is this very comprehensiveness that has given place to an increasingly broad theological spectrum, which is now finding expression within the worldwide communion. The acceptance of all manner of doctrine and practice, combined with the lack of any central adjudicating authority, has brought us to the crisis we are now living through. It is a crisis of competing worldviews: the liberal postmodern worldview vs. the traditional biblical worldview.

As discussed previously, the heresies of our time are monism, pluralism, and relativism, all carefully blended and promoted under the banners of love, tolerance, and social justice. Taken together these form the axis of the liberal worldview, and a foundation for an emerging new one-world religion. This new religious movement has gained traction in the church, and in many cases has already overtaken it. We should not minimize the subtly of this heresy, nor the promotion of it, because it finds expression through the very language of the creeds of orthodoxy.

In contrast, traditional Christianity is based in a biblical worldview that includes: the exclusive nature of salvation through the person of Jesus Christ; a commitment to the objective authority of the Holy Scripture for all times and all places; and the dualism of God as transcendent creator, wholly separate from the creation itself. These stand in direct spiritual opposition to this new liberal religious endeavor, and, in truth, cannot be reconciled with it.

The question now foisted upon the Anglican Communion is, "How do we cope with this situation?" How can we continue to function with two opposing worldviews competing for control in our midst? The answer, simply put, is we cannot. The impossibility of such a task is easily observed in the events of the past few years. We cannot continue this dance of orthodoxy and heresy. Traditional Anglicans are facing a heretical agenda that is intricate and far deeper beneath the surface than the mere "gay bishop" issue. We are facing a theological conflict that is intractable. Further conversation/dialogue/indaba/statements/communiqués and proposed ratification of solutions that are somehow representative of both worldviews is futile.

Re-formation is needed. Re-formation that includes definitive boundaries, a recognized central authority, and which certifies the biblical worldview. The action required is nothing short of formal separation between the competing worldviews and their respective church communities. Naturally, this will bring major changes to Anglicanism, to its polity, to its structures, and to its relationships between member provinces. Some of those relationships will be over; some of those relationships will grow stronger and deeper as we move into the future.

The issue that must be addressed by the Anglican Communion is that of the postmodern worldview growing in its midst, and the corresponding development of a one-world religion. It is an issue of theological meaning and interpretation, of right doctrine and right practice. It is an issue of Christian identity. As Anglicans, it is not enough to simply restate the Lambeth Quadrilateral as the basis of our common life: The Sufficiency of Scripture; Office of the Bishop; Creeds; and Sacraments. Each of these is defined and finds expression from the theological foundation beneath the surface. Differing theologies produce different definitions and answers to the inherent questions being raised. What then is needed for clarity? The kind of clarity which also produces unity, for genuine unity does not exist apart from truth—truth which is acknowledged and agreed upon. There is no division between unity and truth found in the Holy Scripture. The community of believers is unified, because they know the truth and are careful to guard the truth.

Using the cornerstones of the Lambeth Quadrilateral, let us consider that which is necessary to produce truth and unity:

1. Scripture contains all things necessary . . .

This is a lovely sentiment which we would all like to believe in. Yet, simply stating this as fact will not ameliorate the friction within the Anglican Communion, nor solve the ongoing frustrations of the various factions. This is because we have not yet taken the time and done the hard work of defining what we mean by "scripture", nor by what we mean by "sufficient." Thus, two radically opposed worldviews, which have radically different meanings for these terms are able to affirm that yes scripture is sufficient and then go and act out in ways completely at odds with one another. This is because each has a different means of interpretation. In order to resolve this issue, the solution is to take a step further and enact an authoritative method of biblical interpretation—one that is accepted as the standard for all Anglican churches. Only in this manner can we overcome the relativism of the postmodern paradigm, which declares "you have your interpretation and I have mine." Whatever it may be cannot be challenged, because we each put our own meaning into the text.

As Anglicans, we need a clearly defined method of Biblical interpretation, which is in fact biblical! Only by agreeing on such, will we reverse the postmodern premise that the person brings the meaning to the text. The Greek term for this is eisegesis, which is rooted in pride. By agreement on proper guidelines of interpretation as a standard to be adhered to, we reinforce Christian belief in the eternal and living quality of the Word that speaks the truth of God to all generations. We reaffirm the principle of exegesis, which is rooted in humility. Humbly we allow the Word to speak and align our lives to suit what God is saying to us, rather than realigning the Word to suit our lives. A standard for biblical interpretation must include the following principles and presuppositions:

- Meaning and authority are inherent in the Word
- Scripture interprets scripture
- The whole context of scripture always considered with each individual passage
- Proper consideration of genre, redaction, metaphor, poetry and prose, etc.
- Theological method based on Christian worldview
- Essential boundaries of what is or is not considered valid

In addition, the standard must be subject to the councils of the church, reviewed, explained and taught to all members of the fellowship.

2. Creeds are a sufficient statement of faith . . .

The early church began with a simple confession of faith in Jesus as the Messiah—Jesus Christ is Lord. Soon this became expanded in the expression of the Apostles Creed, which articulates a more detailed version of the basic tenets of the faith. This was sufficient for a historical season, but over time new challenges emerged. The church was confronted with heretical positions regarding the person of Christ, which began to become infused into the main of Christian belief and practice. To face these challenges the early church initiated a plan of action that resulted in setting things back in proper order. Their approach was as follows:

A. Gathered together in council

B. Discerned truth from error

C. Declared that which was orthodox (right doctrine)

D. Expanded the Creed appropriately

E. Required assent to remain in fellowship

The result of this process was the production of a restatement of Christian belief in clear and succinct terms, one that corrected false doctrines and set boundaries to prevent their reoccurrence. When further Christological or theological controversies came along, the process above was repeated. For example, the Council of Nicaea expanded the Apostle's Creed to certify Christian truth in the face of Arianism, defining more precisely what was meant by the words describing Jesus as the Son. The Council of Chalcedon further refined the creed in response to the Eutychian controversy, which attempted to redefine the nature of Christ in solely divine terms.

One need only compare the Apostle's Creed with the Nicene Creed to observe this process in operation. Due to theological/ Christological revisions which were popular at the time, nevertheless off track, the council of the church recognized the need to expand and clarify exactly what the creed was saying. In particular, they were careful to define exactly who Jesus is in relation to God the Father. To simply state—"the only begotten"—was no longer sufficient. But now a fuller explanation was required—"God from God, light from light, true God from true God, begotten not made, of one being with the Father. Through him all things were made . . . " This expanded definition was necessary because the foremost heresies that confronted the early church were centered around the person and nature of Christ: modalism, docetism, adoptionism, etc.

So once again, let us consider the process from a broader historical viewpoint:

- Faithful church confesses beliefs through creed
- Heretical thought and teaching gains traction
- Heresies threaten to overtake church community
- Council convenes, discerns truth, and brings correction
   —Orthodoxy restated
   —Creed expanded, clarified, and defined
- Heresy purged
- Assent required to remain in fellowship
- Faithful church confesses beliefs through creed

Clearly, we are living through stages two and three in the present moment, as Anglicans, participating in the Anglican Communion, and indeed, as Christians, participating in the world-wide church. Heretical thought and teaching are threatening to overtake the church. Practices which would have been considered anathema for generations of the faithful are subtly being introduced and celebrated, because they are the new accepted norms for the culture around us. Please understand this is not just an Anglican problem. When I say that the church is at risk, I mean the universal church. If you are reading this from the position of being in a different fellowship in the body of Christ, I mean your church. We are living in a new paradigm.

An underlying principle in operation within the matrix of the new heresy comes from the postmodern view of language and meaning in general. Language is merely the touchstone of experience. Meaning, per se, is not found in the words written; meaning is brought to the text by the reader himself. This is, in my opinion, a classic error of eisegesis, imposing one's own meaning into the text, rather than exegesis, extracting the intended meaning from the text. When this heretical principle is applied to standard statements of Christian belief and practice, such as the creeds, the words, or terms, or language, is retained, but the meanings beneath the words are changed. In fact, it allows for whatever meaning one may deem fit and proper humanly speaking.

For example:

God the Father = The Holy, Transcendent, Creator of the Universe

> First Person of the Trinity
> —*monotheism*
> > *or,*
>
> The divine creative force found within all things and all people
> —*pantheism*
> > *or,*
>
> The universe as a divine conscious thought that contains all things and people within itself
> —*panentheism*

Jesus the Christ = The Incarnate Savior

> Second Person of the Trinity
> —*monotheism*
> > *or*
>
> The apogee of humanity—an enlightened master
> The perfect human who fully realized and participated with the divine within
> > *or/and,*
>
> The one who shows us the way to realize that we are also divine
> —*humanism*

Holy Spirit = Comforter, Counselor, Guide

    Third Person of the Trinity

    —*monotheism*

      or

    The divine evolutionary force which interconnects and motivates the people and events of history all in an ever upward spiral toward consciousness and the goal of divine oneness of all things

    —*monism*

If you are thinking, this sounds a lot like Star Wars, "The force be with you," you are not far off. Star Wars was produced in the nineteen seventies and displays the transition to the postmodern social paradigm. Yet, even Star Wars retains a "dark side of the force", which could be considered sin. Within the definitions of the new postmodern heresy, sin is equated only with ignorance. Sin means that we have not yet gained the knowledge of our participation with the divine within us. Along with the table above, this understanding serves to make the point, that while many can with good conscience confess the same words of the Nicene Creed, each one may be confessing something radically different, and opposed to the meanings assumed there by the Christian church throughout the ages.

    3. Bishops are the overseers of the church . . .

In too many ways the office of bishop has become an exercise of politics. Especially in the West, politically minded clergy rise to the top and put into effect the agenda of their constituents. Even among orthodox dioceses, often the bishop is regarded as the chief pastor, a kind of super rector for the people. I advocate a return to the classic understanding of the episcopate. Bishops are the continuation of apostolic ministry, primarily given to be defenders of the faith. They are to be the chief theologians of the church, with pastoral considerations subordinate. As such, bishops set the standards, enforce the boundaries, and are themselves subject to one another in council, so that error and spiritual malaise do not have place to infect the church.

Anglicans must come to agreement on what the office of bishop entails, and who is eligible to hold such office. In addition, the bishop is the visible connection to the larger fellowship. Thus, the question of how, where, and under what guidelines a college of bishops will be convened, or a council of bishops will operate, especially concerning the discipline of the church by the bishops, and the discipline of bishops by the bishops. These standards need to be clearly articulated. The great gapping hole in the side of a healthy Anglican fellowship is the lack of boundaries and discipline. Anglican comprehensiveness without them does not, and has not, produced Anglican cohesiveness. Conversely Anglican comprehensiveness with boundaries and discipline will equate to Anglican cohesion and health, and would be quite a sight for the world to see.

4. Sacraments convey the grace of God . . .

Sacramental theology has often been a point of contention within the factions of Christianity. One of the strengths of the Anglican-Ism is the willingness to allow for the mystery of God's grace, his presence, and his love to flow through the sacraments of baptism and Holy Communion, without strict human definition. Much of the crisis we now face requires more stringent definition and clarity. However, the sense of the real presence of God in the sacraments goes beyond this kind of endeavor. Nevertheless, we do need to be clear about who God is, the nature of his grace, and the reasons why we as human beings are in need of it.

Sacraments are the means by which God's immanence is made manifest, but this cannot be divorced from his transcendent qualities or everything in worship becomes unbalanced. In the following chapters, I would argue for an expansion of our understanding of the sacramental nature of creation. The principle that all things are available for God to use in manifesting himself could become a theological foundation from which to build unity across denominational lines. In considering the Anglican re-formation ahead, such an understanding of sacramental theology may prove to be a key piece in the revival of the whole.

Throughout this analysis and discussion, we have considered the statement of the Lambeth Quadrilateral—the ways in which it has functioned as a statement of faith for the Anglican Church, and the ways in which it is currently being challenged. The crisis now upon us requires that we move beyond assumed meanings, and establish the criteria necessary for certainty in our beliefs. To set the church back on a sure foundation, let us engage in the same process of the early church:

Convene the Council
  —recognize/discern the heresies that confront us
Clarify, expand, and define orthodoxy—right belief
  —write a clear and succinct statement
Continue as the faithful church in confession
  —let us be certain about what we are confessing

Most importantly we must set appropriate theological boundaries, and enforce the boundaries that are set. Assent to right Christian belief is required to remain within Christian fellowship. Those who are inflicted with heresy and cannot let go of it, the church must let go of them. Pray for them, certainly. Persuade them to return, patiently. However, we can ill afford to continue to waste time and energy, or risk remaining in fellowship with them, without risking the soul of the church in the new one-world paradigm of the twenty-first century.

In truth, we do not have fellowship, in the biblical sense of the word, with those who are caught up in other religions or have put their faith in anyone or anything other than Jesus Christ, as revealed and explained in the Holy Scripture and confessed by the church throughout history. Jesus has commanded us to be compassionate. He did not command us to be tolerant, especially in the way the term is used in the present. Compassion means to suffer along with. Tolerance means to simply leave them to their own devices, however far from God that may take them. As Christians, we are called to speak the truth in love.

Anglican Re-Formation

As we seek to make the transition from talking to acting, and to develop a plan of action, let us keep in mind some key principles in all we consider:

1. Clear definition for all words, terms and concepts
—*meanings can no longer be assumed they must be explained;*

2. Succinct expression of the required components
—*fewer words chosen more carefully will have greater effect for real solutions.*

3. Truth and Unity are inseparable
—*needed to maintain a biblical basis for fellowship*

4. Words must be used only as an incentive for action
—*more words describing the problem will not effect a solution*

The result of the Anglican re-formation of the twenty-first century will be a worldwide church community that will no longer be the Anglican Communion as we know it today. A new community that, I will argue, will even need to be called by a new name. New wine must be put in new wineskins, or else the bottles will break. Perhaps, The Anglican Fellowship of the Christian Church would be a more appropriate description of who we really are in Christ, or rather who we will become.

The Anglican Re-Formation of the Twenty-first Century

In order for the traditional Anglican churches, who are committed to the biblical worldview to flourish, or perhaps even survive, we must commit ourselves to the action of re-formation. Not only for our sakes, but to prepare for our role in the uniting of the Christian church worldwide, which we are moving toward in the future. In the previous chapters I have expounded these ideas more fully, and laid the foundation for that which I assert here. What follows are the actions, processes, and the requirements needed to affect the re-formation and revival of the worldwide Anglican Church:

ANGLICAN RE-FORMATION

1. Acknowledge that Re-Formation is Needed

   Denial is no longer an option, although it is so much easier than actually doing something. Facing the facts, and acknowledging the need are both actions. They are the actions which begin the process of re-formation. To begin, we must recognize that the Anglican Communion is completely mired, bogged down, drowning in a sea of words, and that a new and different approach is the only solution.

2. Gather an Executive Council to Begin the Re-formation Process

   Ultimately, I am advocating that a new Anglican Fellowship be established and governed on a conciliar based model, the churches/provinces in council with one another deciding right doctrine and right practice. In order to set the stage for a larger council of the Anglican churches, an executive council comprised of leaders who are committed to re-formation needs to come together, draft the agenda, and set the plan in motion. The selection of such leadership should not be difficult to discern, as the champions of orthodoxy are well known among us.

   Tasks:

   A. Clarify the Anglican Covenant and include necessary boundaries and enforcement
   B. Establish an authoritative method for biblical interpretation
   C. Write an expanded definition of the terms and concepts found in the creeds to insure proper theological use, and to certify the truth within
   D. Draft a basic statement of belief in the orthodox biblical worldview required for participation in a provincial council, or certify the covenant for this purpose

3. Convene a Provincial Council

   The new Anglican Fellowship will come into being when a worldwide council is convened, which represents the provinces, dioceses, parishes, and various jurisdictions who are willing to commit to the traditional biblical worldview. The council is charged with declaring the right doctrine, orthodoxy, and the right practice, orthopraxis that is acceptable in the Anglican Fellowship of the Christian church. Furthermore, the council must set in place the governing structures and means of relationship between the churches. These structures and relationships must include an accountability to one another that is uncompromising. Autonomy may no more rule the day, for without accountability, boundaries, and a central authority; we may as well stay in the mess we are already in, because that is where we will end up once again.

Tasks:

A. Affirm the commitment and orthodoxy of all who would continue in fellowship

B. Confirm a covenant statement that establishes the Biblical worldview and includes necessary boundaries and consequences—Covenant

C. Set in place a proper governance for the new fellowship

D. Establish a central authority representative of the fellowship to adjudicate on issues of faith and practice—a star council of bishops and theologians which address questions and issues as they arise

E. Separate from the Old Structures of the Anglican Communion

Those who wish to move forward in a decidedly orthodox Christian expression of Anglicanism will be welcomed into participation in the new fellowship. Those who have committed to the liberal postmodern worldview must be left to their own devices. Certainly, we can continue to pray for their repentance. We must act toward them charitably, with compassion, but we no longer can continue joined together with them in communion—"what fellowship has light with darkness?"[1] The world will cry schism. Let them. We must go on proclaiming the gospel, as the new one-world paradigm takes over in place of the postmodern era.

---

1. 2 Corinthians 6:14

The four steps listed above seem simple, yet each one is dense with the actions needed to facilitate the Anglican re-formation of the twenty-first century. Many of the principle strengths of Anglicanism may be retained as we move from the old vessel to the new, and well they should be. We are not abandoning our heritage, rather we are purifying it. It is the weaknesses of Anglicanism which must be jettisoned: the lack of clear boundaries and a central authority which have lead us into the quagmire; the openness to being directed by the belief systems of the surrounding culture which has drawn us away from our calling as the prophetic community of God; and the reliance on structures and solutions based in paradigms gone by which are no longer effective in the emerging one-world era.

Anglican Re-Formation is merely an extended essay from which volumes may be written. Yet, my purpose in writing in the brief time granted to me is to say to all faithful Anglican Christians, "Now is the time to act." I write from the sincere belief that a whole and complete, vibrant Anglican expression of orthodox Christianity will be poised to bring the gospel to the world of this century. Finally, a reformed, revitalized Anglican Fellowship will stand as a central catalyst to connect and unite Christendom in ways we can only begin to imagine.

In Summary

The openness and comprehensive nature of Anglicanism has resulted in the rise of a new religious movement within the Anglican Church, which is based on progressive, postmodern, and monistic theologies that are contrary to the biblical worldview.

The provinces promoting this liberal vision have been and continue to be a integral component of the Anglican Communion, with members participating at every level of leadership, thus effectively blocking any correction from within.

The Anglican Communion is hopelessly mired in a conflict between two competing religions, or worldviews, which are incompatible and irreconcilable, resulting in an endless waste of time and energy expounded in an ongoing stream of dialogue, meetings, statements, and procedures.

Within the existing ethos of the Anglican Communion there exists neither the will nor the means to resolve this crisis, whether by reference to the foundational documents and principles which have comprised our common life, nor by the four instruments of unity charged with ordering our common relationships: The Archbishop of Canterbury; Anglican Consultative Council; The Lambeth; or The Provincial Primates.

The current crisis poses an ever-increasing danger that a worldwide body of Christians who worship together in the Anglican tradition may be lost altogether through disintegration, dissipation, or disillusionment, or even completely overtaken by the postmodern worldview at work within its boundaries.

The time of re-formation is at hand. The need for re-formation of the whole Anglican Communion is acute, and should be immediately acknowledged by all Anglicans formed and committed to a traditional Christian/Biblical worldview. Including: archbishops and bishops; priests and deacon; laity, vestries, and conventions.

Since the Anglican re-formation of the twenty-first century cannot be effected within the polity and structures of the present Anglican Communion, through existing procedures, statements, nor four instruments of unity, new conciliar structures of polity and oversight must be activated. New wine must be put in new wineskins.

Because the existing statements of faith—Holy Scripture, creeds, and Lambeth Quadrilateral while sufficient in meaning in and of themselves, are now subject to the importation of any and all interpretations and theological methods common to the postmodern era, including those radically different and heretical to traditional Christian belief. Therefore, the Anglican re-formation of the twenty-first century must include clear and authoritative guidelines for biblical interpretation, as well as definitions, and meanings correspondent to all statements of belief. Boundaries to be set and enforced among participating members.

Anglican Re-Formation

A new Anglican Fellowship of the Christian church shall be brought into being, that will be committed to an ordering of common life by means of a conciliar polity. Such fellowship will maintain regular councils of all bishops, and/or with other appointed leaders, to discuss the mind of the church. In keeping with the conciliar model, an additional council consisting of one representative from each province will be appointed to act as a central authority within the Fellowship, adjudicating in matters of faith and practice.

The Anglican re-formation of the twenty-first century will not look to itself as the final end of the process, but will continue to seek out and join with other Christian fellowships who, finding themselves in similar circumstances, have committed to upholding the traditional biblical world view. As we move out of the historical paradigm of postmodernity, and shift into the emerging one-world era, the new Anglican Fellowship will seek to be a catalyst for the reunification of Christendom in general, in order that Christians everywhere may join together, as a one-world church comprised of all faithful to Jesus Christ as Lord, and ready to meet the challenge of an emerging one-world religion.

"Worship the Lord in the Beauty of Holiness"
—PSALM 96:9

Chapter 6
The Anglican World

The Anglican-Ism is a global phenomenon. Since the Anglican Church has already spread around the world in the previous historical paradigms, it is now adapting naturally to global interaction. In many ways, Anglicans have been functioning globally with each other for quite some time. Now that interaction is being expanded, as Anglicans are pressed to interact not only with each other, but also with the whole spectrum of church and society.

Paradigm to paradigm the world has shifted, changed, and morphed into new and different modes of being. The monarchial systems of the medieval time gave way to the Enlightenment, and the age of reason in the modern period. As modernity disintegrated into the postmodern period, reason was supplanted by experience as the defining sense of what it means to be human. Now in the one-world era experience has gone viral. Participation reigns as the new mode of being human. We find our identity through everything that we are participating in and with. Participation in all the world has to offer, and indeed, it is all on the table.

While living in the same historical context, much of the Christian church retains a commitment to the faith once delivered to saints. Across denominational lines, the "orthodox" hold fast to the belief in an objective authority of the Bible and the need for regeneration of sinful human nature. Rather than being informed by the prevailing cultural values, many Anglicans, Catholics, and Protestants continue to teach and confess the traditional principles and theology which have been the bedrock of the faith for 2000 years:

- An exclusive view of Jesus as the means of salvation for all mankind
- The inspiration and authority of the Bible in all matters of faith and morality
- The holy and transcendent nature of God
- The need for divine grace to redeem and transform our humanity
- The prophetic witness of the church to the world in all times and places

The conservatism portrayed above stands in stark opposition to the popular revisionism of the Spirit of the Age. This is because each maintains a commitment to a core set of beliefs and practices that are at heart irreconcilable.

A neo-humanism has arisen in the world, which promotes the idea that all are inherently good, or even divine. This increasingly popular viewpoint cannot be reconciled with classical Christian belief in a holy and transcendent God to whom all must give account. Subjective authority derived from the personal experience of the self is in direct opposition with objective authority maintained in the Holy Scripture for all people in every generation.

And so, the conflict has arisen, and the crisis has begun to come to age as we move into the one-world era.

The crisis has only just begun. Anglicans are the canary in the coal mine, gasping for air while worldwide Christianity looks on to see how much oxygen is left. Denial, reconciliation, and détente will not suffice. Re-formation is the only way forward for the Christian church in the midst of one-world. In order to survive, flourish, and proclaim the Gospel, the church must become one as well. This is after all Jesus' prayer for us in John 17:21, "that they may all be one, just as you, Father, are in me, and I in you . . . " The reformation of the sixteenth century brought a splintering of Christianity. It was centrifugal in nature, spinning outward and separating the parts from the whole. The re-formation required in the twenty-first century is just the opposite. It must be centripetal, pulling the pieces back from the periphery to make a cohesive whole.

The two visions which began to come into focus in the postmodern era are each growing stronger and more distinct. If the one-world paradigm is the ultimate melting pot, it is also the ultimate refiners fire. In the same way that the postmodern milieu radicalized the ideals of modernity, one-world dynamics are radicalizing the postmodern theological and moral tenets. Inclusivity, tolerance, and pluralism which were previously amorphous ideals, have become concrete and are taking shape in the institutions and practices of one-world life. Orthodoxy is being pressed upon from every side; called upon to defend its positions; clarify its stance; and articulate precisely the values and beliefs which are essential. Both visions are being melted. Both visions are being refined. As a result, both are emerging stronger and more clearly defined. The question is, "Which one will claim the prize—the soul of one-world?"

Throughout this book, I have sought to further explore the dynamics that have brought us to this historical juncture and continue to drive us forward into the future. As an orthodox Anglican priest, I see clearly the possibility for the Anglican re-formation to become a worldwide re-formation of the Christian church— one that would reunite Christendom in a way not seen since the early church. I believe the calling of the Anglican reformers of the twenty-first century goes far beyond just setting their own house in order. A revived and restructured fellowship of Anglican Churches could readily become a model and a catalyst for the re-formation of the various Christian Fellowships worldwide.

Appendix I

The Chicago-Lambeth Quadrilateral 1886, 1888

Adopted by the House of Bishops, Chicago, 1886

We, Bishops of the Protestant Episcopal Church in the United States of America, in Council assembled as Bishops in the Church of God, do hereby solemnly declare to all whom it may concern, and especially to our fellow-Christians of the different Communions in this land, who, in their several spheres, have contended for the religion of Christ:

1. Our earnest desire that the Savior's prayer, "That we all may be one," may, in its deepest and truest sense, be speedily fulfilled;
2. That we believe that all who have been duly baptized with water, in the name of the Father, and of the Son, and of the Holy Ghost, are members of the Holy Catholic Church;
3. That in all things of human ordering or human choice, relating to modes of worship and discipline, or to traditional customs, this Church is ready in the spirit of love and humility to forego all preferences of her own;
4. That this Church does not seek to absorb other Communions, but rather, co-operating with them on the basis of a common Faith and Order, to discountenance schism, to heal the wounds of the Body of Christ, and to promote the charity which is the chief of Christian graces and the visible manifestation of Christ to the world;

Appendix I

But furthermore, we do hereby affirm that the Christian unity . . . can be restored only by the return of all Christian communions to the principles of unity exemplified by the undivided Catholic Church during the first ages of its existence, which principles we believe to be the substantial deposit of Christian Faith and Order committed by Christ and his Apostles to the Church unto the end of the world, and therefore incapable of compromise or surrender by those who have been ordained to be its stewards and trustees for the common and equal benefit of all men. As inherent parts of this sacred deposit, and therefore as essential to the restoration of unity among the divided branches of Christendom, we account the following, to wit:

1. The Holy Scriptures of the Old and New Testament as the revealed Word of God.
2. The Nicene Creed as the sufficient statement of the Christian Faith.
3. The two Sacraments—Baptism and the Supper of the Lord—ministered with unfailing use of Christ's words of institution and of the elements ordained by Him.
4. The Historic Episcopate, locally adapted in the methods of its administration to the varying needs of the nations and peoples called of God into the unity of His Church.

Furthermore, Deeply grieved by the sad divisions which affect the Christian Church in our own land, we hereby declare our desire and readiness, so soon as there shall be any authorized response to this Declaration, to enter into brotherly conference with all or any Christian Bodies seeking the restoration of the organic unity of the Church, with a view to the earnest study of the conditions under which so priceless a blessing might happily be brought to pass.

> *Note: While the above form of the Quadrilateral was adopted by the House of Bishops, it was not enacted by the House of Deputies, but rather incorporated in a general plan referred for study and action to a newly created Joint Commission on Christian Reunion.*

The Chicago-Lambeth Quadrilateral 1886, 1888

Lambeth Conference of 1888
Resolution II

That, in the opinion of this Conference, the following Articles supply a basis on which approach may be by God's blessing made towards Home Reunion:

a. The Holy Scriptures of the Old and New Testaments, as "containing all things necessary to salvation," and as being the rule and ultimate standard of faith.

b. The Apostles' Creed, as the Baptismal Symbol; and the Nicene Creed, as the sufficient statement of the Christian faith.

c. The two Sacraments ordained by Christ Himself—Baptism and the Supper of the Lord ministered with unfailing use of Christ's words of Institution, and of the elements ordained by Him.

d. The Historic Episcopate, locally adapted in the methods of its administration to the varying needs of the nations and peoples called of God into the Unity of His Church.

Appendix II

Anglican-Ism Terms and Characters

Thomas Wolsey: An ambitious colleague of King Henry VIII who rose in power to the rank of cardinal and papal legate over all the English bishops. Wolsey asserted his power in all walks of society, and supported the cause of education. However, Wolsey's exercise of power fostered "antipapalism and anticlericalism". Eventually he ran into conflict with Henry over the divorce of Katherine, and was charged with treason, but died before trial.

King Henry VIII: Bold, ambitious, audacious King of England. Henry ruled through the power of persuasion and ingenuity, utilizing the parliament to pass laws against those who opposed his will, and convincing the populace that he had their best interests at heart. Henry facilitated the breach with Rome in order to secure his divorce from Katherine and subsequent remarriage to Ann Boleyn, naming himself as "Protector and Supreme Head of the English Church and Clergy." He magnified the office of Archbishop of Canterbury and appointed Thomas Cranmer to the position. He dissolved the monasteries which had been a central feature of English Christianity for hundreds of years, to appropriate their income for the crown. Henry VIII remained ostensibly catholic in doctrine, but may have had affinity for the growing reform movement. He revolutionized the constitution of the Church of England and effectively severed its subordination to Rome.

Anglican-Ism Terms and Characters

William Tyndale: As the ideas of the reformers gained influence in the early 1500s the demand for an English Bible increased. William Tyndale took up the task of printing and distributing copies of the Bible in English. Forced to flee to Germany he continued his work smuggling the Bible to England in bales of wool. His addition of protestant commentary to the Scripture, eventually resulted in his death-condemned as a heretic.

Thomas Cranmer: The reform minded Archbishop of Canterbury during the reign of Henry VIII. Cranmer sought to unify the worship in the Church of England, and produced the Book of Common Prayer. The BCP retained elements of both catholic and protestant theology, rejoicing the moderates but drawing criticism from conservatives (catholic) and reformers (protestant). Under Edward VI, Cranmer solidified his reformed views, so that when Mary became Queen, and initiated the Catholic revival, he was tried and executed as a heretic.

The English Prayer Books (1459, 1552): Known as the Book of Common prayer they were written and published by Thomas Cranmer. The prayer books sought to bring liturgical reform and continuity of worship to the English Church. Just prior to their publication a wide variety of worship expressions could be found, some severely lacking in content. The first prayer book retained much of the catholic Sarum Rite, while the second, under reformation influence, made significant changes to affirm protestant doctrines-especially regarding the nature of the Eucharist.

Mary Tudor: ascended to the throne of England upon Edward VI death in 1553. Mary was a devout Catholic who had lived for 20 years in exile in France. She immediately set out to undo the breach with Rome, and nullified the enactments of Henry VIII. Mary nearly succeeded in returning England to the Roman Catholic fold, but her marriage to the king of Spain, and the spirit of nationalism and reform already part of English life, caused her to fail.

Appendix II

Elizabethan Settlement: The reestablishment of the Church of England by Elizabeth as a distinct body apart from Rome. Elizabeth reversed the policy of Mary, who sought to return the church to papal oversight, and charted a Via Media, which retained catholic polity while affirming protestant reforms—especially communion in both kinds and married clergy. The settlement asserted the queen as "Supreme Governor" of the English Church.

John Jewel's Apology: argued in favor of the Elizabethan Settlement. Jewel appealed to scripture and the early church, asserting that the Church of England was truly catholic. His arguments for England and against Rome were published in *Ecclesia Anglicana and Apologia Ecclesia Anglicana*.

Richard Hooker's Laws of Ecclesiastical Polity: Hooker was educated by John Jewel, and continued the intellectual work of establishing the Anglican Church. Hooker "sought to provide Anglicanism with a philosophical and logical basis" in his book, *On the Laws of Ecclesiastical Polity*. He refutes a growing puritan influence in England, which asserted that Scripture is the only test of what is correct. Hooker believed that the Church could make laws as long as they did not contradict scripture.

William Laud: Chancellor and Archbishop under Charles I (1629–1640), whose passion for reform often bordered on severe. Laud was closely aligned with the king, and asserted his power against all manner of irregularities in the church. He sought to unify the church by means of strict enforcement of the law, and saw himself as "born to set other people right." He demanded obedience to the BCP by the bishops, and used the courts to enforce his authority.

The Caroline Divines: a group of writers and scholars who continued in the tradition of Jewel and Hooker. They sought to provide to the world a viable description of the Anglican Church, thus establishing an intellectual basis for the life of the church. In particular they sought to ground the Church of England in the tradition of the early church apart from Rome,

Anglican-Ism Terms and Characters

maintaining its catholic nature and witness to the Apostolic faith: Lancelot Andrews, George Herbert, John Cosin, Jeremy Taylor, Nicholas Ferrar.

Oliver Cromwell: the Puritan member of the house of commons, who became master of England. Cromwell formed a cavalry after civil war broke out in 1642, and quickly defeated troops loyal to the king. After the king was defeated, Cromwell took the reins of power as Lord Protectorate and set about religious reforms that sought to make room for "Presbyterians, Baptists, Independents, and even some moderate advocates of episcopacy." He attempted to make England into a republic, but failed to do so in the end.

Cambridge Platonists: a group of scholars primarily members of Emmanuel College, a center of the Puritan community, who appealed to reason as the deliberator of religious strife. They sought to find harmony between philosophy and religion, and espoused a mystical spirituality devoted to prayer and meditation. They sought after a pure and holy life, and the reconciliation of all truth with the Spirit of God.

Latitudinarians: originally a term for the Cambridge Platonist, it was later applied to those who succeeded them. A school of liberal, rational men who deplored the religious enthusiasm of their times and sought to use reason as a means of attaining a quiet ordered society. They set high standards of morality and charity, devoting themselves to good works and tolerance of other Christians.

Non-Jurors: a group of about four hundred clergy who refused to acknowledge the appointment of William and Mary as sovereigns over England. The Non-Jurors believed strongly in the Divine Rite of Kings. Therefore, when James II was deposed, yet remained alive, they would not compromise their loyalty for conscience sake. This resulted in their deprivation, and schisms in the church when their offices were reappointed.

The SPCK & SPG: Two religious societies formed in 1698 and 1701 respectively, devoted to the spread of the Gospel and the work of the church overseas. The Society for Promoting Christian Knowledge provided religious literature abroad, and founded libraries and schools. The Society for the Propagation of the Gospel sought to establish the church in the colonies and convert the native peoples.

Deism: a religious philosophy based upon nature and reason. Deists retained God as the original Creator, but removed all involvement on His part after the finished work. Special revelation, i.e. the work of Christ, was ignored in favor of a non-demanding faith in reason and the understandability of the universe.

John Wesley: Anglican priest who, following an unsuccessful mission to Georgia, was converted through an encounter with God at a Moravian Pietist gathering on Alderstreet. During the reading of Paul's Epistle to the Romans, Wesley felt his heart "strangely warmed" and recognized God's personal gift of salvation through Jesus Christ. Wesley preached this "New Birth" experience all over England, often outdoors to the masses with dramatic results. His follow up Bible study groups became known as the Methodist movement

George Whitfield: a contemporary of Wesley dubbed the Divine Dramatist. Early in life Whitfield studied to be an actor, but upon his conversion set out to preach the Gospel. He traveled to America and preached with astonishing results up and down the Atlantic seaboard. A gifted and powerful orator, he preached in the open air to crowds numbering into the thousands. Thus, he initiated the first Great Awakening in American history.

John Henry Newman: Leader of the Oxford Movement, a group of scholars who sought to reform the church from without. Newman wrote tracts exhorting a return to catholicity, especially that of the early church fathers. In protestant England Newman and the Tractarians met much resistance for their dislike of the reformers, and advocating of Roman Catholic doctrine. Eventually, Newman left the Church of England and became a Catholic himself.

Anglican-Ism Terms and Characters

F.D. Maurice (1805–72): an early modern scholar who was brought up as a Unitarian, but ordained in the Church of England. His teachings were rationalistic, pantheistic, and anti-dogmatic. He believed that God's revelation meant the unveiling of His nature by degrees, and that everlasting punishment referred to punishment administered in eternity not lasting forever.

The Lambeth Conferences: Anglican General Council of Bishops, begun in 1867. In the nineteenth century worldwide growth of the Anglican Communion presented problems that needed to be addressed. The success of the early conferences in defining the unity of the church, and addressing its concerns, led to regular conferences thereafter. They provide opportunity for decisions on church polity and theology, as well as fellowship between bishops. Lambeth magnified the office of Archbishop of Canterbury.

Lux Mundi: a volume of theological essays published in 1889, written by clergy in favor of the Labor Movement. The essays were intended to provide a justification of Christian Socialism. This resulted in the formation of the Christian Social Union which worked for brotherhood and justice for all men.

Edinburgh Conference: An interdenominational gathering of missionaries and mission agencies in 1910. The conference fostered cooperation on the mission field, and addressed problems pertaining to such. From this gathering the Ecumenical movement was born, facilitating greater cooperation amongst various denominations.

William Temple: Archbishop of Canterbury 1942. Temple was involved in the birth of the Ecumenical movement, which lead to the formation of the World council of Churches.

Arthur Michael Ramsey: Ordained Archbishop of Canterbury in 1961. He was confronted with growing administrative burdens in the church along with rapid changes. Ramsey presided at Lambeth 1968 and had earlier met with the pope to initiate a dialogue toward full communion.

Bibliography

Barth, Karl. *Church Dogmatics.* Edinburgh: T&T Clark Ltd., 1961
Bloesch, Donald, *Toward a Theology of Word.* Downers Grove: Intervarsity, 1992
Book of Common Prayer, BCP. New York: Church Hymnal Corporation, 1979
Brooks, Peter Newman. *Thomas Cranmer's Doctrine of the Eucharist.* London: Macmillan Academic and Professional LTD, 1992
Chadwick, Owen. *The Mind of the Oxford Movement.* Stanford: Stanford University Press, 1967
Chan, Simon. *Spiritual Theology.* Downers Grove: Intervarsity, 1998
Downers Grove, IL: Intervarsity Press, 1992
Christian Classics Ethereal Library. http://www.ccel.org/ccel/wesley/journal.vi.ii.xvi.html
Duffy, Eamon. *The Stripping of the Altars.* New Haven and London: Yale University Press, 1992
Fairfield, Les. *Lecture on Richard Hooker.* Ambridge, PA: Trinity Episcopal School for Ministry, 2001
Foster, Richard. *Streams of Living Water.* San Francisco: Harper Collins, 1998
Gonzalez, Justo L. *The Story of Christianity-Vol.* 2.San Francisco: Harper Collins, 1985
Grenz, Stanley J. & Olson, Roger E. *20th Century Theology.*
Jewel, John. *An Apology of the Church of England.* New York: Cornell University Press,1963
Lewis, C.S. *Mere Christianity.* New York: Harper Collins, 1980
McFague, Sallie. *Models for God.* Minneapolis: Fortress, 1987
McGrath, Alister. *Evangelical Distinctives.* Downers Grove: Intervarsity, 1995
Moorman, John. *A History of the Church of England.* London: Adam & Charles Black, 1976
Niebuhr, Richard. *The Kingdom of God in America.* Middleton: Wesleyan University Press, 1988; Harper and

Bibliography

Parsons, Donald J. Some *Theological and Pastoral Implications of Confirmation, Confirmation Re-Examined.* edited by Kendig Brubaker Cully. Wilton, CONN: Morehouse-Barlow Co., 1982

Payne, Leanne, *The Healing Presence.* Grand Rapids: Baker Book House, 1989

Robinson, J.T. *Honest to God.* SCM Press LTD, 1963

Roman Catholic Church. *Catechism.* Online: http://www.scborromeo.org/ccc.htm

Schleiermacher, Friedrich. *Speeches on Religion to its Cultured Despisers.* Cambridge: Cambridge University Press, 1988

Spong, Bishop John Shelby. 12 *Theses.* Online: http://en.wikipedia.org/wiki/John_Shelby_Spong

Stott, John. *The Anglican Synthesis: Essays by Catholics and Evangelicals.* edited by W. R. F. Browning: Derby, Peter Smith 1967

Sykes, Booty, and Knight. *The Study of Anglicanism.* Minneapolis: Fortress Press 1998

Wainwright, Geoffrey. *Christian Initiation: Chapter 3.* Richmond: John Knox Press, 1969

Willard, Dallas. *The Divine Conspiracy.* San Francisco: Harper Collins, 1998

Wright, N.T. *What St. Paul Really Said.* Grand Rapids: Eerdmans, 1997

Yates, Arthur S. *Why Baptize Infants?* Norwich: Canterbury, 1993

www.ingramcontent.com/pod-product-compliance
Lightning Source LLC
Chambersburg PA
CBHW070929160426
43193CB00011B/1628